# GROWING POINTS IN THEOLOGY

## SAMARITANS AND JEWS

Also in this series:

# SAMARITANS AND JEWS

The Origins of Samaritanism
Reconsidered

R. J. COGGINS

*Lecturer in Old Testament Studies, King's College, London*

JOHN KNOX PRESS
ATLANTA, GEORGIA

# For Palma, Sarah and David

© Basil Blackwell 1975

*American Edition published by*
*John Knox Press, Atlanta, Georgia*

*Library of Congress Cataloging in Publication Data*


Coggins, R. J.  1929–
  Samaritans and Jews.

  (Growing points in theology)
  Bibliography: p.
    1. Samaritans—Religion—Relations—Judaism. 2. Judaism—Rela-
tions—Samaritan. 3. Bible. O. T.—Criticism, interpretation, etc.
I. Title
BM915.C63      296.8'1      74-3712
ISBN 0-8042-0109-9

*Printed in Great Britain by*
*The Camelot Press Ltd, Southampton*

# Contents

# Abbreviations

| | |
|---|---|
| AB | Anchor Bible |
| *ABR* | *Australian Biblical Review* |
| *ANET* | *Ancient Near Eastern Texts relating to the Old Testament* edited by J. B. Pritchard |
| *AOTS* | *Archaeology and Old Testament Study* edited by D. Winton Thomas |
| ASTI | Annual of the Swedish Theological Institute in Jerusalem |
| ATD | Das Alte Testament Deutsch |
| AV | Authorised Version |
| *BA* | *Biblical Archaeologist* |
| *BWANT* | *Beiträge zur Wissenschaft vom Alten und Neuen Testament* |
| *BWAT* | *Beiträge zur Wissenschaft vom Alten Testament* |
| *BZAW* | *Beihefte zur Zeitschrift für die Alttestamentliche Wissenschaft* |
| *CQR* | *Church Quarterly Review* |
| *DOTT* | *Documents from Old Testament Times*, edited by D. Winton Thomas |
| *HTR* | *Harvard Theological Review* |
| IB | Interpreter's Bible |
| ICC | International Critical Commentary |
| *IDB* | *Interpreter's Dictionary of the Bible* |
| *IEJ* | *Israel Exploration Journal* |
| *JAOS* | *Journal of the American Oriental Society* |
| *JBL* | *Journal of Biblical Literature* |
| *JCS* | *Journal of Cuneiform Studies* |
| *JJS* | *Journal of Jewish Studies* |
| *JNES* | *Journal of Near Eastern Studies* |
| *JSS* | *Journal of Semitic Studies* |
| *JTS* | *Journal of Theological Studies* |
| *KS* | *Kleine Schriften* |
| *LXX* | *Septuagint* |
| MT | Massoretic Text |
| NEB | New English Bible |
| *NTS* | *New Testament Studies* |
| *RB* | *Revue Biblique* |
| *RGVV* | *Religionsgeschichtliche Versuche und Vorarbeiten* (Berlin) |
| RSV | Revised Standard Version |
| RV | Revised Version |
| *TGUOS* | *Transactions of the Glasgow University Oriental Society* |
| *VT* | *Vetus Testamentum* |
| *VTS* | *Supplements to Vetus Testamentum* |
| *ZAW* | *Zeitschrift für die Alttestamentliche Wissenschaft* |

# I

# Introductory

## The Nature of the Problem

'Jews have no dealings with Samaritans.' These well-known words from the traditional English versions' rendering of John 4:9, describe a state of affairs which was apparently well established in the first century A.D., and has lasted almost to our own times. (One of the happier consequences of the 'six-day war' of 1967 has been that the main surviving group of Samaritans, on the traditional site of Mount Gerizim, have been able to join once more with other smaller groups at Holon, near Tel-Aviv, in Israeli territory, and that their relations with the Israeli authorities have apparently been amicable.) The meaning of the statement in the Fourth Gospel does in fact raise greater difficulties than might at first sight appear, and these will be considered in due course.[1] Nevertheless, what is depicted there is a relationship even more vividly portrayed in the stories of the Good Samaritan or of the Ten Lepers in the Gospel of Luke (Luke 10:29ff.; 17:11ff.). C. K. Barrett aptly summarizes the situation by his comment that this 'is not (as is generally supposed) an explicit statement about general relations between Jews and Samaritans, but it does in fact attest the common attitude of Jews to their neighbours, which was one of suspicion. The Samaritans were (not exactly enemies but) seceders and nonconformists.'[2]

It has, of course, long been assumed that we have knowledge

---

[1] See below, p. 139 f.
[2] C. K. Barrett, *The Gospel according to St. John* (London 1955), pp. 194f.

of the Samaritans from a much earlier period than this; that the Old Testament as well as the New has information to offer us; and that we could explain the historical development of this hostility between Jews and Samaritans to a large extent from the biblical evidence. In the English versions the word 'Samaritans' is found in the Old Testament only at 2 Kings 17:29, and this chapter has normally been taken as the starting-point of their history. A brief summary would run something like this. After the Assyrian conquest of the Northern kingdom of Israel, the inhabitants of the land were deported, never to return (the 'ten lost tribes'). In their stead, the land was repopulated by groups brought from other parts of the Assyrian Empire—groups whose race was as mixed as their religion, which was a syncretistic blend of their own local cults and a debased version of Yahwism. By contrast to all this, when the Jews of Judah and Jerusalem were exiled, following the invasion by the Babylonians under Nebuchadnezzar, they remained a homogeneous group. No foreign settlers were brought in to occupy their land, and they were allowed to return to Jerusalem and rebuild their temple within seventy years. From then on, the Jerusalem community remained as a self-contained entity, avoiding contact with their paganized neighbours as far as possible. The books of Haggai, Ezra and Nehemiah illustrate some of the tensions thereby brought about, while the *Antiquities* of Josephus attest other details, such as the building by the Samaritan community of the rival temple on Mount Gerizim which, on this traditional view, represented the final breakdown of any relations between Jews and Samaritans.

Such, basically, is the picture of Judaeo-Samaritan attitudes provided by a *prima facie* consideration of the Old Testament material. For a long time, even after the beginnings of the period of critical biblical scholarship, it was supposed that this picture of the Samaritans as a people of mixed race and religion was to all intents and purposes an accurate one. Thus, to take a characteristic example from the early years of this century, the first edition of *Hastings' One-Volume Dictionary of the Bible* (1909), in the article 'Samaritans' by R. A. S. Macalister, describes them as 'the descendants of the Cuthites, Avvites, Sepharvites and Hamathites, established by Sargon in Samaria after he had put an end to the Israelite kingdom. They were instructed in a form of the

Hebrew religion (which they grafted on to their own worships) in order to appease the "God of the Land".' The article goes on to speak of an 'admixture of heathen worship' which was still traceable in New Testament times.[3] Descriptions of this type owe a great deal to later Jewish polemic; in particular, they owe as much to Josephus' *Antiquities* as to the Old Testament itself. Especially noteworthy here, as we shall see, is the use of names like 'Cuthites' as an apt description of the Samaritans.

In general, it is only in extreme conservative circles that this is still regarded as a plausible picture of Samaritan origins. But there are exceptions. J. Bright's *History of Israel*, for example, has rightly become a standard treatment of its subject, yet his view of the events described in 2 Kings 17 is surely over-simplified. He states, as if it were simple history, that 'these foreigners brought their native customs and religions with them and, together with others brought in still later, mingled with the surviving Israelite population. We shall meet their descendants later as the Samaritans.'[4] This only differs from the older view in so far as it acknowledges that some at least of the native Israelite population did remain in the land.

We shall return to further consideration of the story in 2 Kings 17, but at this point we may notice as appropriate the description of that chapter in another recent history of Israel—that of R. E. Murphy, in the *Jerome Bible Commentary*, who speaks of it as 'a many-sided theological meditation'.[5] This is an important judgement, in that it gives a pointer to one of the main reasons why the traditional picture set out above is no longer acceptable as it stands. One of the many sides in that meditation of which 2 Kings 17 consists is a strong polemical element, and this is a factor which, as we shall see, appears to have influenced both Jewish and Samaritan accounts of their early history. The general recognition of the fact that the historical witness of the Old Testament needs to be used with considerable caution has led to a number of modifications which characterize many recent accounts of Samaritan origins. The word 'modifications' is deliberately chosen, for in general it is a modified rather than a completely

[3] Op. cit., p. 821a.
[4] *A History of Israel* (2nd ed., London, 1972), p. 274.
[5] *The Jerome Bible Commentary* (London, 1968), II, p. 684.

different picture that has been drawn. (As will be seen later, there are a few scholars who have started from the Samaritans' own account of their origins, rather than from the Jewish side; but for the moment our concern is with the proper understanding of the Old Testament material.) Two points in particular have remained characteristic of many descriptions: the view of Samaritanism as a debased form of religion, containing many syncretistic elements; and the notion of a schism—with its twofold connotation, of a definite break that took place at a specific moment in history, and of that break as implying the departure of the schismatic from the accepted norm. The date of such a schism is now commonly held to be later than the eighth century, which was the appropriate date on the older view outlined above, and various periods have been suggested, and various events characterized, as the occasion of the schism: the sixth century, associating it with the return of the Jerusalem Jews from exile in Babylon; the fifth century associating it either with the opposition to Nehemiah or with the rigorist racial policy of Ezra; the fourth century, associating it with the building of the Samaritan Temple on Mount Gerizim. More detailed presentations of these and some other reconstructions of Samaritan origins will be considered in the course of this study; but these features—the allegedly syncretistic nature of Samaritanism, and the idea of a schism as a breaking-away from mainstream Judaism at a definite point in time—still underlie much of the discussion. It is hoped that it will become clear that neither of these features should be taken for granted as truly characteristic of the situation.

The main point of this study is to attempt a fresh examination of Samaritan origins, and the greater part of it will naturally be concerned with references, real or supposed, to the Samaritans. Before beginning a more detailed consideration along these lines, however, it is important to notice that the traditional picture outlined above has been much modified in respect of its description of the Jews' own history. That picture is in its main outlines based on the viewpoint of the Chronicler, and the account of the exile and return in 2 Chronicles and Ezra is now generally recognized as being an idealized one. Few have gone so far as C. C. Torrey who held that such Jews as were exiled to Babylon would not have been able to form any kind of organized and coherent community,[6] yet the picture of Judah lying desolate for seventy years (2 Chron. 36:21) until it was repopulated by a mass return of exiles from Babylon (Ezra 2) is now generally held to be a theological interpretation of the significance of this period rather than an accurate historical representation.[7]

Certain of the more obvious ways in which this new evaluation of the history of the Jews affects our understanding of the Samaritans may briefly be noted. The Old Testament shows clear evidence of a tendency to exaggerate both the number and the importance of those taken into exile in Babylon, by the development from the figures given in Jeremiah 52:28–30, where the total number involved is the relatively modest one of 4,600, to the statement in 2 Chronicles 36:20f., where all who survived the destruction of Jerusalem were taken to Babylon, the land being left desolate.[8] It is a matter of current dispute whether those who remained in Judah (and all would now agree that there were some such) continued to exercise a significant role. M. Noth, for example, maintained that 'though . . . very important developments in life and thought took place among those deported to Babylon, which were to influence the whole later history of Israel, nevertheless even the Babylonian group represented a mere outpost, whereas Palestine was and remained the central arena of Israel's history',[9] and it has been held that the Deuteronomic circle in particular continued to be active in Palestine during this period.[10] These points remain in dispute, but certainly the Chronicler's view is an idealization. This has important implications for our understanding of the history of this period. When the Chronicler's view has been taken literally, it has commonly been held that the only remaining inhabitants of

[6] This reinterpretation of the history of Israel in the sixth century B.C. was worked out in several of Torrey's studies. On this specific point, see for example *Pseudo-Ezekiel and the Original Prophecy* (New York, 1970 (1930) ), p. 33.

[7] Many of the theological and historical issues of the crucial sixth-century period are discussed in P. R. Ackroyd, *Exile and Restoration* (London, 1968).

[8] For a discussion of the various numbers of exiles given in the Old Testament and in Josephus, see Ackroyd, op. cit., pp. 23ff.

[9] *The History of Israel* (London, 1958), p. 295.

[10] For a critique of this view, see E. W. Nicholson, *Preaching to the Exiles* (Oxford, 1970), especially ch. 4.

the land must have been the Samaritans, who must therefore have been the adversaries of the loyal Jews mentioned in Ezra and possibly also in Haggai.

The Chronicler's idealization has not only affected the picture of the exile, but has also exaggerated the eagerness with which those in Babylon returned to Judah when opportunity was offered. Part of the Chronicler's purpose clearly was to establish that the Jerusalem community of his time was the true Israel; around it was gathered the whole range of ancient tradition, as is shown especially in Nehemiah 9; the role of David as the chosen one of Yahweh is greatly stressed; and it was important to emphasize that the whole community had been through the purifying experience of exile and had returned from it to rebuild the temple and to resume the whole of those cultic requirements which placed them in a right relation with their God. Whether or not it is proper to describe part of the Chronicler's purpose as anti-Samaritan polemic is a question which will arise later; but we can certainly state that he upholds very positively the special position of Jerusalem.

This general picture will need to be borne in mind when we examine particular aspects of the history in greater detail. One other preliminary point should also be made at this stage. This concerns the great upsurge of interest in Samaritanism. With notable exceptions, little interest was taken in and even less was known about the Samaritans by European scholars before the beginning of the present century; only the Samaritan Pentateuch had come in for careful examination on account of its value in textual criticism (just as earlier it had been used by Protestant and Roman Catholic writers in their attacks on each other concerning biblical inspiration.[11] In more recent years this situation has changed very considerably. Much Samaritan manuscript material has been edited and published; a number of scholarly works dealing with different aspects of Samaritanism have appeared. As is so often the case in such situations the availability of new material does more to raise fresh problems than to solve old ones, yet the Samaritans' own view of their past is no longer all owed

[11] For an outline account of these controversies, see J. D. Purvis, *The Samaritan Pentateuch and the Origin of the Samaritan Sect* (Cambridge, Mass.; 1968), pp. 73–5.

to go by default in attempts to reconstruct the course of their history.

In this respect we may notice at the outset that the Samaritans place the irrevocable division which has separated them from the Jews as early as the eleventh century B.C., at the time of Eli. It is thus noteworthy that the traditions of both groups imply that there was a definite schism, and that it took place at a date earlier than seems acceptable on the evidence now available. It will be argued here that many modern writers, while not accepting these extreme views, have also tended to date the division too early. It will also be argued that no sudden dramatic event, but an extended period of increasingly embittered relations, seems best to account for the estrangement that developed.

The main part of this study will therefore be devoted to a consideration of the evidence provided by the Old Testament and other Jewish literary sources, by archaeology, and by what is known from the Samaritan side—both their own chronicles and ancient allusions to Samaritanism—in an attempt to understand and trace more fully this process of estrangement. It is clearly impossible to take account of more than a small proportion of previous explanations of this situation, but at least the attempt can be made to comment on a representative selection of earlier views. Even at the outset it can be stated that many of the conclusions will be negative, in the sense that many supposed references to Samaritanism turn out on closer examination to be nothing of the kind, and few dramatic or decisive events can be pinpointed as leading to a division between Jews and Samaritans. But even negative conclusions have their value if they warn against the danger of tying up loose ends too neatly, and if—as it is hoped will be the case—they serve as reminders of the rich variety and complexity of Judaism in the last pre-Christian centuries.

Perhaps, too, it may be possible to isolate and examine some of the misunderstandings and confusion that have constantly recurred in discussions of Samaritanism; and it is to one such cause of confusion—the appropriate names for the two communities—that we must first of all turn, before examining afresh the traditional evidence from ancient sources.

## 'Jews' and 'Samaritans'

If any reminder were needed of the importance of getting names straight, it has been provided by a frequent experience during the preparation of this study. Within the last few years the word 'Samaritan' has changed its meaning in common English usage, and now normally signifies the organization whose efforts are directed to giving counsel and support to those tempted to commit suicide. Surprise has several times been expressed that the origins of that group were so obscure as to need investigation, and the appropriate explanation has been necessary.

That particular cause of confusion can easily be remedied, but there are more deep-rooted difficulties in talking about both Jews and Samaritans which have often occasioned misunderstanding and frustration. It has always been notoriously difficult to define what exactly is meant by 'Jew', though for most practical purposes the identification has been clear enough, both in the ancient world and in more recent times. Two points should, however, be borne in mind. First, the English word is derived through the classical languages from the Aramaic and Hebrew *yehudai/yehudi*, that is, an inhabitant of, or a member of the tribe of, Judah. One of the roots of Judaeo-Samaritan antagonism was the tribal and geographical opposition illustrated by this fact. To examine the north–south tensions within Israel throughout the Old Testament period would be to go well beyond the limits of the present study, but they will certainly need to be borne in mind when considering Jews and Samaritans. The second point arises out of this, and concerns the usage adopted here. Some ambiguity will be almost inevitable, since at times the word 'Jews' will be used specifically of those to whom and by whom the Samaritans were opposed; while at other times the suggestion will be made that Samaritanism must be seen within the wider phenomenon of Judaism. This is admittedly inconsistent usage, but no natural alternative appears to be available, and it can only be hoped that misunderstanding will not thereby be caused.

Problems of a different kind surround the proper naming of the Samaritan community, and here the ambiguity has often been of considerable importance in contributing to the disputes surrounding their early history.[12] It has already been noted that in the English versions the word 'Samaritans' is found only at 2 Kings 17:29. This translates the Hebrew *haššōmᵉrōnîm*, which has become Σαμαριται in the LXX, and the familiar English form is derived from the Greek. But the basic meaning of this word seems simply to be 'inhabitants of Samaria' (Hebrew: *šōmᵉrōn*), and it will become apparent throughout this study that the Samaritans are associated not with Samaria but with Shechem. The Samaritans themselves make a clear distinction between their own forebears and the inhabitants of Samaria. Thus, for example, in that part of the Samaritan Chronicle II which corresponds to 1 Kings 16, the biblical account of the founding of Samaria by Omri is followed by an extended note which explains that the inhabitants of Samaria and its daughter-cities were called *'Shomronim* after the name *Shomron'*,[13] and this distinction is characteristic of the Samaritan Chronicle. It has not been so carefully maintained in many modern discussions, partly because no appropriate word has been adopted with the meaning 'inhabitants of Samaria'. The word 'Samarians' has been suggested and is sometimes used in this sense, but it has not become widespread, and the result has been a continuing cause of confusion. In many recent accounts of the post-exilic period, it is not easy to decide whether the writer is unaware of the ambiguity in the use of the term 'Samaritans', or whether a deliberate assertion is being made that the Samaritans should not be distinguished from the inhabitants of Samaria.

If we turn from current usage to ancient practice, some interesting developments emerge. We have already noted that the word *haššōmᵉrōnîm* occurs only at 2 Kings 17:29, and that its natural meaning is 'inhabitants of Samaria'. It will be argued in subsequent sections of this work that there are no unambiguous references to the Samaritans in the Hebrew Old Testament, and part of the support for this argument is the very fact that none of the terms

[12] On the names given to the Samaritan community, see M. Gaster, *The Samaritans* (Schweich Lectures, London, 1925), pp. 4f., and H. G. Kippenberg, *Garizim und Synagoge*, RGVV, XXX (Berlin, 1971), esp. p. 33, note 1.

[13] *Samaritan Chronicle II*, 1 Kings 12–22, I, A*–F*, edited by J. Macdonald, p. 163. (The rather complex method of reference to the Chronicle is that used by Macdonald.) For fuller treatment of this Chronicle, see pp. 117–31 below.

descriptive of the later Samaritan community are found there. Various divisions arose within the Jewish community centred on Jerusalem; there were a number of occasions of conflict between that community and different external enemies. In no case are the terms used to describe these divisions and conflicts those which would later be used of the Samaritans, at least in the Old Testament itself, though such an identification is made in some instances by Josephus.

When we turn to the Apocrypha, clear references to the Samaritans are found, notably in Ecclesiasticus 50 and 2 Maccabees 5 and 6. Though there may well have been a polemical element in each of these passages, the Samaritans are not referred to by any distinctive name but simply described as 'the foolish people that dwell in Shechem' (Ecclus. 50:26), or as 'the people who dwell in Gerizim' (2 Macc. 6:2). Josephus, though his terminology is usually different, on occasions also speaks of 'Shechemites' (e.g. *Antiquities*, XI, 342), a usage which has been explained by some scholars as indicating a Shechem or Samaritan source.[14]

In general, however, Jewish descriptions of the Samaritans from approximately the beginning of the Christian era have a more markedly hostile tone. The use, for example, by Josephus, of Σαμαρῖται (the same as the LXX of 2 Kings 17, 29) seems now to imply a contemptuous association with the by this time paganized city of Samaria (e.g. *Ant.* IX, 290). More usual, both in Josephus and the Mishnah, is the description 'Kuthim', and this indicates even more clearly than the use of Σαμαρῖται that the story of 2 Kings 17 was by this time being applied to the community at Shechem, for Kuthah was the place of origin of one of the groups described as having been introduced into the land by the king of Assyria (v. 24). By such a description, the charge against the Samaritans of heathen origins and syncretistic practice would be furthered. It will be seen that the inappropriateness of the name is matched by the falsity of the accusation.

So much for Jewish descriptions of the Samaritans. What of the Samaritans' own self-designation? They frequently refer to themselves or their ancestors simply as 'Israel', but where, as often, this title might cause misunderstanding, they describe

---

[14] See Kippenberg, op. cit., pp. 53ff., and Appendix B to the Loeb edition of Josephus, *Antiquities*, vol. VI, pp. 498–511.

themselves as '*šāmᵉrîm*', their form of the Hebrew '*šōmᵉrîm*
that is, 'keepers' (sc.: of the Torah). This usage is regularly found
in their Chronicle II, but as will be noted when that Chronicle
is considered in fuller detail,[15] the date of any part of the work
is extremely difficult to estimate. The earliest certain reference to
this title appears to be in the *Panarion* of Epiphanius of Salamis,
written *c*. A.D. 375,[16] but, though the Samaritan Chronicle usage
almost certainly goes back earlier than this, precision in dating is
impossible. It would certainly appear that the two titles *šōmᵉrōnîm—
šāmᵉrîm* were adopted in connection with one another, but which
came first and which is the reaction, is not possible to decide.

The suggestion has sometimes been made that there is one Old
Testament allusion to the Samaritan self-designation. In 2 Chronicles 13, in the context of war between Abijah of Judah and
Jeroboam I of Israel, Abijah makes a speech of the kind which
the Chronicler often puts into the mouth of those for whom
Yahweh is fighting. At v. 11 he condemns the Northern Israelites
with the phrase 'we are keepers (*šōmᵉrîm*) of the charge of Yahweh
our God, but you have forsaken him'. W. Rudolph suggested that
this part of 2 Chronicles, placed immediately after the division
of the kingdom, was intended as 'the "magna carta" of the Jewish
monopoly of salvation, the "sermon on the mount" of Abijah',[17]
and he regarded this claim as really being aimed against the
Samaritans contemporary with the Chronicler. The point was
carried a stage further by M. Delcor, who pointed out that the
particular emphasis of the speech was on the true priesthood being
maintained at Jerusalem, whereas Northern Israel had illegitimate
priests serving false gods.[18] It is certainly the case that one of the
great divisions between Jews and Samaritans concerned the nature
of true priesthood, but it must for the moment remain an open
question whether the Chronicler's polemic should be so narrowly
defined. As for the use of the term *šōmᵉrîm*, the coincidence with
later custom is certainly striking, but in the complete absence of

[15] See pp. 117–31 below.
[16] Cf. Kippenberg, op. cit., p. 34.
[17] W. Rudolph, 'Problems of the Books of Chronicles', *VT*, IV, 1954,
p. 404.
[18] M. Delcor, 'Hineweise auf das Samaritanische Schisma im Alten
Testament', *ZAW*, 74, 1962, pp. 283f.

other evidence, it must remain very doubtful whether such usage was already an established fact at the time of the Chronicler.

One other point should, however, be noted about the Samaritan self-designation. Their devotion to the Torah was already recognized from the fact that it alone constituted their canon of Scripture, and this emphasis is furthered by the word *šām$^e$rîm*—they were self-consciously the real keepers of the Torah. The very name, that is to say, implies a group which maintained the traditional ways and was suspicious of change, and this is indeed characteristic of much that we learn about the Samaritans. Within the broad spectrum of Judaism they represent a conservative old-fashioned element—certainly not the syncretism of which they are condemned by their Jewish neighbours. Furthermore, the stress on the Torah is suggestive for the date at which the community took its distinctive shape, for it was in the last pre-Christian centuries that this veneration for the Torah reached its height. Such probably late Old Testament material as Psalm 119 and the Book of Daniel, and outside the Old Testament the whole tradition of Pharisaic Judaism illustrate the point. Already, therefore, the names used both by the Samaritans themselves and by those who were hostile to them give some indication of the background from which they emerged.

# 2

# The Witness of the Old Testament

*The Period of Assyrian Domination*

We have already noted at the very outset of this study that the story in 2 Kings 17 is no longer widely regarded as a straight-forward account of Samaritan origins. Nevertheless, that chapter remains as the appropriate starting-point for our consideration of the whole question of Old Testament references to the Samaritans, both because of the traditional view that has been taken of the story, and also because its indirect importance is still considerable. Thus, for example, J. D. Purvis, in his important study of Samaritan origins, *The Samaritan Pentateuch and the Origin of the Samaritan Sect*, has recognized the polemical character of the chapter, but can still treat it as the basis for our knowledge of 'the actual state of religion in Samaria following the Assyrian conquest'.[1] Already we notice the ambiguity with regard to the relation of the Samaritans to Samaria.

Our first consideration in examining 2 Kings 17 must be the fact that all modern critical studies of the books of Kings recognize that they cannot be regarded simply as 'objective history' (whatever that may be!) but are written to express a particular understanding of God's purpose and his dealings with his people, illustrated through the events of their past. The viewpoint expressed is usually regarded as Deuteronomic. From time to time the setting-out of the course of events in the books of Joshua, Judges, Samuel and Kings is interrupted by a kind of sermon, drawing out the lessons of the events that have been described. These sermons are

[1] Purvis, op. cit., p. 94.

characteristic of the Deuteronomic viewpoint both in language and style and in theological outlook.[2] Such a sermon is to be found in 2 Kings 17.

The opening verses describe the conquest of Samaria by the Assyrian forces, and the problems which they raise concerning the date and the identity of the Assyrian king who was responsible for the final overthrow of the city need not concern us here. Vv. 7–23 then draw the moral that is to be learnt from these events. Despite all that Yahweh has done for his people, Israel had continued to sin and brought condemnation upon herself; punishment was therefore inevitable. This sermon, clearly intended for the southern audience to whom the books of Kings were addressed, is most probably to be seen either as a warning that similar punishment would be inflicted upon them if they did not mend their ways, or, perhaps more likely, as an explanation of why they had already been punished in a like fashion. In any case, where these verses are concerned with the North, it is the old Northern kingdom, not the Samaritans in any later sense, which is the centre of attention. It is also noteworthy that these verses are markedly free of any anti-Northern bias.

The part of this chapter which has in the past been taken as an account of the origin of the Samaritans is the last section, vv. 24–41.[3] The previous section ended with a statement of the exile of Israel to Assyria (v. 23), and this seems to be the starting-point for the expansion found in the following section. This section itself betrays more than one viewpoint, and it is possible to speak here of different 'sources' without attempting to make precise judgements upon the nature—literary or otherwise—of such sources. The first is in vv. 25–8 with the possible addition of v. 32 and is characterized by the fact that it condemns not Samaria nor the Samaritans of Shechem, but Bethel, where it is alleged that a polluted form of Yahwistic worship was maintained. It should thus be regarded as being in line with a number of other

---

[2] This interpretation of the Former Prophets owes much to M. Noth, *Überlieferungsgeschichtliche Studien* (Halle, 1943), pp. 3–110. It has been much discussed in subsequent studies; for a recent treatment, see Ackroyd, *Exile and Restoration*, pp. 62ff.

[3] A fuller examination has already been given by the present author in 'The Old Testament and Samaritan Origins', *ASTI*, 6, Leiden, 1968, pp. 37ff.

passages in the Old Testament which regarded Bethel as *the* centre of schism (1 Kings 12 and 13; Amos 7:10ff.; Jer. 48:13); it throws no light on the Samaritans. At first sight, the second source, which should probably be regarded as consisting of vv. 29–31 and 34b–40, seems more promising, with its use of the name *šōmᵉrōnîm* (v. 29) and its description of the importation of foreign settlers. Neither of these points, however, will bear the weight that is sometimes put upon them. With regard to the first, we have already seen that *šōmᵉrōnîm* should not in the first instance be taken as having any further meaning than 'inhabitants of Samaria'. As to the second point, the basic reference in these verses is not so much to the native inhabitants as to those who were introduced into Israel by the imperial authorities of Assyria. A. Alt has warned against the danger of confusing the representatives of the imperial authorities with the native population (of whom, as will shortly be seen, the vast majority must have remained in the land), and both here and on a number of subsequent occasions it was with the imperial representatives at Samaria that the Jerusalem Jews found themselves at loggerheads.[4] Sometimes such tension arose over what we would describe as political differences; here, it was syncretistic religious practice which was held against these alien groups, when they attempted to combine the continuing worship of their own gods with what was thought to be appropriate for the local deity. It is possible that the activities in the religious field of Nehemiah in his second mission (Neh. 13:23ff.) were motivated by a similar state of affairs.

It would appear, therefore, that this chapter offers no internal evidence in favour of the view that it was concerned with the origin of the Samaritans. There are a number of pieces of external evidence which point very clearly in the same direction. The point has several times been noted, for example by H. H. Rowley,[5] that in those parts of the Old Testament which can be dated in the period between the fall of Samaria and that of Jerusalem, there is no reference to the North in terms which suggest the existence in

[4] A. Alt, 'Die Rolle Samarias bei der Entstehung des Judentums', *KS*, II (Munich, 1964), pp. 313–37.

[5] H. H. Rowley, 'The Samaritan Schism in Legend and History', in *Israel's Prophetic Heritage*, edited by B. W. Anderson and W. Harrelson (Preacher's Library, London, 1962), p. 209.

the old Northern kingdom of a group in any sense identifiable with the later Samaritans. It is noteworthy, too, that the Chronicler, for whom the books of Kings were a primary source, made no use of this chapter save for a brief note which is irrelevant to our present concern in 1 Chronicles 5:25f. This could be interpreted in two ways, which are not mutually exclusive; either the 2 Kings story had not yet been reinterpreted in an anti-Samaritan sense, or the purpose of the Chronicler was not so specifically anti-Samaritan as has sometimes been alleged.

These considerations for the understanding of 2 Kings 17 are arguments from silence; perhaps more remarkable is the fact that the Samaritans in their Chronicle II made free use of it in their interpretation of their own history.[6]

Yet it is beyond dispute that this chapter did come to be understood in an anti-Samaritan sense. When did this process begin? Our earliest witness appears to be Josephus. Here as elsewhere he elaborates the underlying Old Testament material, and in his treatment of the fate of the Northern kingdom and its inhabitants there are a number of such elaborations (*Ant.*, IX, 277–91). In particular he describes the new inhabitants of the land as χουθαιοι, and elaborates on their origin in Kuthah (located by Josephus in Persia). He stesses that the syncretistic rites have continued to be practised down to his own time; that the Samaritans are the descendants of these pagan immigrants; and that they only wish to be associated with the Jews when they see that the Jews are prospering. We cannot tell how much earlier than Josephus this tradition of interpretation went; it may well be that it was comparatively recent in his time, for it accords well with other examples of anti-Samaritan polemic which we shall have cause to notice from the beginning of the Christian era.

We need not, therefore, expect to find any direct testimony bearing on Samaritanism in the period of Assyrian domination. Some brief consideration must nevertheless be given to the state of affairs in the territory of the former Northern kingdom during that period, both to provide further corroboration of the picture provided by 2 Kings 17, and also because of its significance for the understanding of later developments in the area. Such extrabiblical material as is relevant will first be considered, and then

[6] Macdonald's edition, p. 177.

attention will be given to the Old Testament material which appears to have a bearing on this period.

Our starting-point is the often-quoted extract from the Annals of Sargon relating to the fall of Samaria and the subsequent deportation. The claim there made is, 'I surrounded and captured the city of Samaria; 27,290 of the people who dwelt in it I took away as prisoners'.[7] There has sometimes been a tendency to allow a degree of credence to extra-biblical figures which is not accorded to those in the Old Testament itself, but at least it seems unlikely that the Assyrian king would have underestimated the number of his captives. That Sargon was responsible for the deportation is generally agreed, though there is dispute whether the actual capture of the city was achieved at the beginning of his reign or at the end of that of his predecessor, Shalmaneser V.[8] As already observed when considering 2 Kings 17, there is no need here to enter into detail concerning the capture of Samaria. We may simply note that it is likely that the large-scale deportations were carried out by Sargon in consequence of the widespread revolts which took place in 720.[9]

The question then arises: what proportion of the population of the country is likely to have been involved? To arrive at any kind of accurate estimate in matters of this kind is notoriously difficult, for demography was an unknown science in the ancient world, but various cautious estimates have been made. Thus, R. de Vaux suggested a total population at this period of something under 800,000.[10] If this is at all accurate it would imply the deportation of between 3 and 4 per cent of the population.[11] Not much stress

[7] The numbers vary slightly in different versions of the Annals. Those quoted are from the Display Inscription (D. J. Wiseman in *DOTT*, p. 60; A. L. Oppenheim in *ANET*, pp. 284f).

[8] Further consideration of the historical problems associated with the Assyrian capture of Samaria and its consequences can be found in H. Tadmor, 'The Campaigns of Sargon II of Assur', *JCS*, XII, 1958, pp. 22–40, 77–100, and W. W. Hallo, 'From Qarqar to Carchemish: Assyria and Israel in the Light of New Discoveries', *BA*, 23, 1960, pp. 34–61.

[9] Tadmor, art. cit. Noth, *History of Israel*, p. 262.

[10] R. de Vaux, *Ancient Israel* (London, 1961), p. 66.

[11] This is slightly lower than the estimate of H. G. May, 'The Ten Lost Tribes', *BA*, 6, 1943, pp. 55–60, who suggested a figure around 5 per cent (p. 58).

can be placed on the actual wording of the Assyrian annals, but they would suggest—and the circumstances of a siege would bear out—that the majority of the deportees would have been the inhabitants of Samaria itself, no doubt including many who had gone there as refugees during the siege. For the most part it will presumably have been the upper classes who were affected, since they would be more readily identifiable as potential leaders of resistance.[12] In the place of those deported, we need not doubt that settlers were brought from other parts of the Assyrian Empire, as is stated in 2 Kings 17, but it is clear that the native Israelites continued to form the overwhelming majority of the population. Some inter-marriage there may have been, but it is clear that the distinction between the indigenous inhabitants and those whose primary loyalty was to the current imperial power continued long after the eighth century. The Samaritans' self-portrait in their Chronicle at this point is clearly shaped by later ideas of a righteous remnant, who 'did not deviate from the way of the holy law, nor did they worship other gods. They did not behave as the nations did, nor did they forsake the chosen place Mount Gerizim Bethel, but they continued to worship the Lord their God.'[13] However much of an idealization this may be, it is at least clear that the religious features of later Samaritanism show no sign of any syncretism brought about by a mixture between native Israelites and those whom the Assyrians brought into the country.

This separation between the native Israelites and the settlers was considered by Alt to have been so complete that the life of the native population would have been little affected, and he maintained that the period after the fall of Samaria was in fact the time of the compilation of Deuteronomy.[14] Such a thesis raises considerable difficulty,[15] but even so we should not go to the other extreme and suppose that no independent religious life could be carried on in the North after the fall of Samaria. The books of Kings picture Judah as if she were independent at this

[12] Noth, 'The Jerusalem Catastrophe of 587 B.C.', in *The Laws of the Pentateuch and Other Essays* (Edinburgh, 1966), p. 263.

[13] *Samaritan Chronicle II*, 2 Kings–2 Chronicles, H. (Macdonald's edition, p. 178).

[14] Alt, 'Die Heimat des Deuteronomiums', *KS*, II, pp. 250–75.

[15] For a criticism of this view see E. W. Nicholson, *Deuteronomy and Tradition* (Oxford, 1967), pp. 80f.

time, and northern Israel as if it had altogether ceased to exist; but each of these presentations may be seen as exaggerations, designed to give sharper emphasis to the Deuteronomic theology: Manasseh was presented as a free agent and so his sins would appear even more heinous; northern Israel lay desolate, and so her sinfulness could be seen to have received its due punishment. In fact, though Manasseh was allowed some nominal measure of independence, the situation in North and South must have been basically very similar. Samaria then became a province of the Assyrian Empire after its capture, being added to the existing Palestinian provinces of Dor, Megiddo and Gilead, which had been established at the time of Tiglath-Pileser III. Some of the names of Assyrian governors of Samaria have survived.[16] The basic structure of this provincial system appears to have extended right through the Babylonian and into the Persian period, a fact which will become significant when we consider the later history, but we have no further detail as to the history of the province from extra-biblical sources. (The Samaritan Chronicle, which might have been expected to throw some light on the period, betrays considerable chronological confusion at this point, as will be seen when we examine it in greater detail.)

Within the Old Testament itself, there is a small number of passages which bear in some way on the state of affairs in the North at this period. The most important is the description in 2 Chronicles 30 of Hezekiah's dealings with the North. Though the assessment of its significance must to some extent depend on our total picture of the work of the Chronicler, some consideration may be given to the historical situation which it reveals. At times, of course, it has been denied that any historicity can be discerned behind this story.[17] Nevertheless, it seems now to be widely agreed that, though a measure of idealization has taken place so as to model Hezekiah's preparations for the Passover on the requirements of the P stratum of the Pentateuch, it is also

[16] Alt, 'Das System der Assyrischen Provinzen auf dem Boden des Reiches Israel', *KS*, II, pp. 188–205; Noth, *History of Israel*, p. 263.

[17] 'Probably a purely imaginary occurrence', E. L. Curtis, *The Books of Chronicles*, ICC (Edinburgh, 1910), pp. 470f. Many other commentators have taken a similar view: see Bright, *History of Israel*, 2nd ed., p. 281, note 39.

inherently probable that the king would have taken advantage of the disturbances in the Assyrian Empire at the time of the accession of Sennacherib (705) to attempt to extend his influence into the North. This dating, however, must remain conjectural; while one approach to these events would see them as providing part of the background to Sennacherib's siege of Jerusalem, another suggestion has been that the religious reform probably took place soon after the accession of Hezekiah.[18]

If we assume some activity on Hezekiah's part in the northern territory, while recognizing that the purpose of this story is not primarily that of giving an historical account of the events of his reign, what do we learn of significance for our present study? Several interesting points emerge. In the first place, it is noteworthy that while Hezekiah received a favourable response from some of those in the more distant areas of Asher, Zebulun and part of Manasseh, those nearer at hand, that is presumably in Ephraim, rejected his overtures (vv. 10f.). (The version of these events given in the Samaritan Chronicle implies a complete rejection; but the setting of the story is very different, and it will be considered more fully later.) Different reconstructions of this varied response are possible. It could be argued that his picture of rejection by the Ephraimites simply represents polemic against the later inhabitants of that area, in which case Hezekiah's message to them (vv. 6ff.) would really be aimed at the northerners of the Chronicler's own time; as Bright has remarked, 'Hezekiah addresses the northern Israelites as if they were the later Samaritans!'[19] On the other hand, it is quite plausible to suppose that there were historical reasons for this different response: those Ephraimites who wished to do so had already undertaken the comparatively short journey to Jerusalem, or possibly Ephraim was under stricter Assyrian surveillance than the more scattered northerly areas.[20]

Another possible pointer towards this involvement by Hezekiah in the northern situation has been suggested by H. J. Kraus.[21]

---

[18] So J. M. Myers, *II Chronicles*, AB (New York, 1965), p. 176. For a general survey of the problems involved in this period, see H. H. Rowley, 'Hezekiah's Reform and Rebellion', in *Men of God* (London, 1963), pp. 98–132.

[19] Op. cit., p. 281.     [20] Myers, op. cit., p. 178.

[21] H. J. Kraus, *Worship in Israel* (Oxford, 1966), pp. 61ff.

He is sceptical whether any historical basis underlies the story in
2 Chronicles, and suggests that the story reflects cultic controversies
in the third century between the Jerusalem community and the
Samaritans. The unusual date of this celebration—'in the second
month' (v. 2)—was in accordance with the provision made in
Numbers 9:9ff. that the Passover might be so celebrated in case
of defilement—the defilement in this case being, of course, the
worship on Mount Gerizim which the Jerusalemites regarded as
false. The tradition recorded in 1 Kings 12:32f. of the Northern
festivals being held a month later than the corresponding observance in the South may also be relevant here. This whole theory
is an interesting one, and certainly the shaping of the story of
Hezekiah's Passover, with its similarities to Josiah's Passover as
recorded in 2 Kings 23, suggests that the historical element here
may be less than elsewhere in the account of Hezekiah. Whether
a specifically Samaritan interpretation is correct seems doubtful;
Kraus achieves the identification by postulating a third century
date for the Chronicler, which is later than that usually held,
and by supposing that the Samaritan 'schism' had already taken
place by that period, though he himself admits that there is no
evidence for a separate Samaritan community until a later period.
Another feature in this reconstruction which gives rise to some
doubts is that it would present the Samaritans as rejecting Jewish
offers of reconciliation, rather than vice versa, which was the more
familiar situation. There are, therefore, difficulties about this
interpretation of the story; it may nevertheless be regarded as a
possible clue to the background of the Chronicler.

Finally, some scholars have seen a further pointer to Hezekiah's
northern interest in the fact that his son Manasseh was given the
name of the eponymous founder of a northern tribe, and it has
been suggested that Manasseh's wife was herself from Galilee.[22]
But evidence of this kind really amounts to very little, since so
little of the accompanying circumstances is known.

To summarize our consideration of 2 Chronicles 30, we may
regard it as likely that Hezekiah did indeed show an interest in
the territory of the northern kingdom, possibly with a view to
restoring the borders of his territory to those of David, at a time
of hoped-for Assyrian weakness; that religious reform may well

[22] Bright, op. cit., p. 281.

have been associated with this, though the terms in which it is described are to a considerable extent a reading back from the norms of a later period; and that any reference there may be in this chapter to the Samaritans has its point in the situation contemporary with the Chronicler rather than that of the eighth century.

We may deal more briefly with a number of other biblical passages which allude in some way to the state of affairs in the North at this period. In 2 Kings 18, the summary account of the fall of Samaria in vv. 9–12 is in substantial agreement with the picture given in 17:1–23, both in its theological assessment and in the date and description of the place of exile. A greater problem is raised by v. 34, which the RSV, following MT closely, renders: 'Where are the gods of Hamath and Arpad? Where are the gods of Sepharvaim, Hena and Ivvah? Have they delivered Samaria out of my hand?' Many commentators have emended the text, claiming the support of the parallel passage in Isaiah 36:19, which omits the reference to Hena and Ivvah, and of some LXX texts and the Vetus Latina, which add, 'Where are the gods of the lands of Samaria?'[23] But, whatever may have been the original form of this text, its present wording is surely significant: it looks like an interpretation perhaps by the same hand as was responsible for 17:24–41 as we now have it, with the implication that those in whom the contemporary northerners trusted were the gods of those alien places from which they had come. Placed as it is within the context of the Rabshakeh's speech, it must remain uncertain whether it is to be taken simply as anti-northern polemic or whether it reflects a tradition (seen in 2 Chronicles 30 but not otherwise alluded to in 2 Kings) according to which Hezekiah had intervened in the North so that Sennacherib had then to reconquer it. In any case it is clearly implied that the gods of the northerners were those of the heathen settlers—what J. A. Montgomery called 'a clever insertion in condemnation of heathen Samaritanism'.[24]

---

[23] J. Gray, *I and II Kings*, Old Testament Library (London, 2nd ed., 1970), p. 677.

[24] J. A. Montgomery, *I and II Kings*, ICC (Edinburgh, 1951), p. 490. Montgomery states that the suggestion goes back to A. Rahlfs, *Septuaginta Studien*, III (1911), p. 278.

Another biblical passage which is significant for our understanding of this period is Isaiah 7:8b. It is almost universally agreed either that the text should be emended or that this passage is a gloss, for in its present form it would have been little consolation to Ahaz to know that Ephraim's destruction could be expected sixty-five years hence. No satisfactory emendation has been suggested, and it seems probable that we have here to reckon with a gloss, inserted after the time of Isaiah, but not so much later that the historical 'norm' of the complete destruction of the northern kingdom had already been established. It would seem, therefore, that the glossator knew of an event *c.* 670 (that is, about sixty-five years after the Syro-Ephraimite war, which provides the basic context of Isaiah 7), which he regarded as even more decisive in its effects for Northern Israel than the fall of Samaria itself had been. There are no allusions to such an event in 2 Kings, but it is possible that the suggestion (which goes back to Archbishop Ussher in the seventeenth century) should be adopted, that the same event is referred to in Ezra 4:2, where 'the adversaries of Judah and Benjamin' claim that they had worshipped the same God as the Jerusalem Jews 'ever since the days of Esar-haddon king of Assyria who brought us here'.[25] Ezra 4 raises many problems, some of which will be considered later, but at least some suggestion is here offered of a continuing tradition of further deportations during the seventh century, and a further warning against regarding the fall of Samaria as implying the complete desolation of the whole territory which the account in 2 Kings 17 implies; conditions remained more fluid, both in the political and the religious sphere, than we might at first suppose.

Another passage in Isaiah which has been regarded as relevant to Judaeo-Samaritan relations is 11:10–16, which has been taken by O. Kaiser[26] as dating from the third century and as having for its background 'the Samaritan schism [which] had broken the last links between north and south'. Such an interpretation is possible, though the expression seems somewhat misleading, both

[25] O. Kaiser. *Isaiah 1–12,* Old Testament Library (London, 1972), p. 94. The account in Esar-haddon's Annals of his last campaign in the West, in 671, may allude to this. He describes his march through Palestine from Tyre to the Brook of Egypt (*ANET,* p. 292).

[26] Op. cit., p. 165.

in its reference to a schism and also in the implied absence of continuing links, but we should bear in mind that hostility between North and South is a widespread Old Testament theme and hope for their reconciliation is also so general that precision in dating such a passage as this may be unattainable.[27]

It is not until the reign of Josiah (640–609) and the decline of Assyrian power that the biblical evidence affords us a somewhat fuller picture. Three aspects of Josiah's reign are relevant for consideration here: his expansion into the territory to the North; his religious reforms, both in Jerusalem and in the North; and the finding of the book of the law. The chronological and causal inter-relation of these events remains in dispute, and since it is not strictly relevant to our present purposes, each of these aspects will be considered in turn without any attempt to prejudge the other issues.

It has been widely suggested in recent years that either Josiah himself or the compilers of the biblical accounts of his reign pictured his expansion into the northern areas in terms of the restoration of the Davidic empire. 'Josiah had the master-picture of David's empire before his eyes—it is possible that he regarded himself as the second David promised by Jahweh.'[28] However this may be, the opportunity for Josiah to realize his ambitions in practice came with the breakdown of Assyrian authority in Palestine, which followed the death of Assur-banapal, none of whose successors was able to establish himself against Median and Babylonian revolts, which culminated in the fall of Nineveh and the final collapse of Assyria in 609. The account of this extension of Josiah's power is found in 2 Chronicles 34, without any precise parallel in 2 Kings. It is impossible to be certain at what stage in Josiah's reign it took place—the attempt by F. M. Cross and D. N. Freedman to work out a precise chronology based on a supposed move towards independence following the death of Assur-banapal, dated by them in 633[29] has not been universally accepted, some

[27] Kaiser himself draws attention to the presence of similar hopes in Jeremiah (3:18) and Ezekiel (34:23; 37:15ff.).

[28] G. von Rad, *Old Testament Theology*, vol. 1 (Edinburgh, 1962), p. 76. Similarly Noth, *History of Israel*, p. 273.

[29] F. M. Cross and D. N. Freedman, 'Josiah's Revolt against Assyria', *FNES*, XII, 1953, pp. 56ff.

regarding the likely date as being rather later, others maintaining that such precision is impossible to attain.[30] In any case, however, the fact of this expansionist policy of Josiah is generally accepted, and there is some archaeological evidence to support it. The ostrakon found at Yavneh-yam, in the North, shows that for a time at least Josiah exercised control there.[31] What remains uncertain is the extent of any resistance that Josiah may have encountered—Noth suggests that 'Presumably the governors of the provinces affected put up as much resistance as they could, with the help of the newly established foreign upper classes',[32] but this is based on what is *a priori* likely to have been the case rather than on any specific evidence. Nor do we know the extent to which the provincial structure itself was affected. It did not disappear, for it persisted in basically similar form in the Babylonian and Persian periods. (Another of Alt's suggestions, that the Judahite boundary-lists in Joshua 15:21ff. reflect the situation under Josiah has been followed by some other scholars, but other dates have also been proposed.[33]) But whether or not Josiah's control ever effectively reached Naphtali in the far North (2 Chron. 34:6), the very fact that it was at Megiddo that he met his death shows something of the extent of his claim to rule, not only in the territory adjoining Judah, but also in what had been the Assyrian province of Galilee. At the risk of labouring the point, we observe that in all this activity there is neither any place found for a group comparable to the later Samaritans (whose own Chronicle makes no mention of Josiah's expansion to the North), nor is the impression sustained that there had been a once-for-all settlement of the affairs of the North.

The second aspect of Josiah's policy is his religious reforms. The impression created by 2 Kings 22 is that the reform was dependent upon the finding of the book of the law, but according

[30] Nicholson, *Deuteronomy and Tradition*, pp. 9ff.

[31] J. Naveh, 'A Hebrew Letter from the Seventh Century B.C.', *IEJ*, 10, 1960, pp. 129ff.

[32] Noth, *History of Israel*, pp. 273f.

[33] Alt, 'Judas Gaue unter Josia', *KS*, II, pp. 276–88. Cf. F. M. Cross and G. E. Wright, 'The Boundary Lists of the Kingdom of Judah', *JBL*, 75, 1956, pp. 202–6, where a ninth-century date for these lists is proposed—a view which has itself been disputed by other scholars. No consensus of opinion has emerged.

to 2 Chronicles 34 the reform was already in progress when the law-book was found, and this view of events is now widely accepted as historical.[34] As a slight variant on either of these views, Noth has argued that the section describing the reform (2 Kings 23:4–20) is unrelated to the account of the finding of the law-book and should be regarded as 'an annalistic account of the measures taken by Josiah in the cult-political sphere . . . more especially the step-by-step elimination of all Assyrian cults'.[35]

There is general agreement, therefore, on the historicity of Josiah's religious reforms, even if their relation to other events in his reign remains in dispute. The account of these reforms contains, as we should by now expect, certain polemical features. We may note first of all that neither here nor elsewhere in 2 Kings is reference made to Shechem, the home of the later Samaritans. It is indeed true of the Old Testament generally that there is no overt anti-Shechemite polemic until we reach Ecclesiasticus 50:26, with the doubtful exception of Hosea 6:9. There it is not clear whether those condemned for their crimes 'on the way to Shechem' should be associated specifically with the city itself. It might be that the phrase 'they murder on the way to Shechem', which fits somewhat awkwardly into its context, is itself a later anti-Samaritan gloss.[36] Elsewhere references to Shechem of any kind are very rare—a fact which M. Gaster saw as suspicious in itself: 'It is not difficult to draw conclusions from this fact; it was the desire of obliterating every reference to the seat of the hated Northern Sanctuary.'[37]

To return to the reforms of Josiah: not only Shechem passes unmentioned, there is no condemnation of contemporary Samaria. The only reference, to 'the cities of Samaria' in 23:19, seems clearly to refer to the imperial province rather than to the city itself, and appears to be an annalistic note introduced to justify Deuteronomic

[34] So e.g. Rowley, 'The prophet Jeremiah and the Book of Deuteronomy', in *From Moses to Qumran* (London, 1963), p. 196.

[35] Noth, *The Laws in the Pentateuch*, p. 42.

[36] Different interpretations of this passage are offered by Nicholson, *Deuteronomy and Tradition*, p. 63 and note 2, and by E. Nielsen, *Shechem* (Copenhagen, 1959), pp. 289ff. A. Phillips, *Ancient Israel's Criminal Law* (Oxford, 1970), p. 101, suggests that the reference may be to Shechem as a city of refuge, to which access was being prevented by the priests.

[37] Gaster, *The Samaritans*, p. 11, note 1.

hostility to the ways of the old Northern kingdom rather than showing any specific reference to a new state of affairs as described in c. 17. It is once again against Bethel that the main attack is directed. Both in v. 4, where practical difficulties are ignored in the description of what has been described as the action of 'a perfect Deuteronomist' against 'the basest altar of all',[38] and in the passage describing the destruction of the high-place of Bethel (vv. 15–20), it is the apostasy of Bethel and the perfection of Josiah's work which is the main theme. It is possible that the same source as was noted in 2 Kings 17:25–8 should be traced here. In any event, the total picture is not of a division which could be expressed in terms of Jews and Samaritans, but rather of Yahweh-worship being carried on at a variety of local shrines, much as it had been right through the period of the divided monarchy. Rowley's comment is apt: 'This is not to suggest that religious conditions in northern Israel were satisfactory after the fall of Samaria any more than they had been earlier, or any more than they continued to be in the southern kingdom. It is but to say that there is no evidence that they were seriously worsened by deportations.'[39]

Finally, it is necessary to notice briefly the significance of the event most particularly associated with Josiah's reign—the finding of the book of the law (2 Kings 22:8ff.). That this was either the whole or some part of our present book of Deuteronomy seems to be one of the established results of Old Testament scholarship which continues to withstand the attacks made from time to time against the identification.[40] The acceptance by the Samaritans of Deuteronomy as 'scripture' in the fullest sense lends further support to the view that no decisive break between Jews and Samaritans can be held to have taken place by this period. Indeed just as the Samaritans fully accept Deuteronomy, so that book refers to the sacred mountain of the Samaritans, Gerizim, with no disapproval (Deut. 11:29; 27:12). Indeed, the suggestion has been made on a number of occasions that the original intention of

---

[38] N. H. Snaith, in IB, III (New York, 1954), p. 320.

[39] Rowley, *The Samaritan Schism in Legend and History*, p. 210.

[40] There are many treatments of the various aspects of this problem: see, for example, the survey of views in Nicholson, *Deuteronomy and Tradition*, ch. 1.

CSJ

the compilers of Deuteronomy—now commonly held to have come from the North—was that the one sanctuary would be at Shechem.[41]

Significant in this connection is the mutual attitude of the northerners and the former Prophets, Joshua–2 Kings. These books are not part of the Samaritan canon of scripture, but this should not be put in terms of 'rejection'. A Samaritan book of Joshua has long been known, and the Samaritan Chronicle II, to which reference has already been made, includes extensive parts of all these biblical books. Within the books themselves there is a clear attitude of hostility towards the North, both to the very fact of the existence of another kingdom which was regarded as schismatic, and also more specifically to the worship at certain shrines which was regarded with particular abhorrence. As we have already seen, this applied especially to Bethel—no mention is made of Shechem. This somewhat complex inter-relation will need to be borne in mind when we come later to consider the way in which the Samaritans regarded themselves as distinct from what they called the 'eight tribes' of northern Israel. For the moment, we need only raise one question with regard to this attitude of hostility. If the Deuteronomic movement had its origins in the North, and if the Former Prophets in their completed form are essentially the product of a Deuteronomic group, why should there be such hostility toward the North? Part of the answer might be that there is here a kind of convert's zeal against old associations, and an anxiety to uphold the claims of Jerusalem as the place which Yahweh had chosen. But whatever the cause of this hostility, it was essentially aimed against the alleged evils of the old Northern kingdom; it cannot be construed as an attack upon Samaritanism.

## The Sixth-Century Prophets

There is a sense in which it might be claimed that the argument in the preceding section is unnecessary, since the view that 2 Kings 17 can be taken as an accurate historical record of the origins of Samaritanism is not now often held. Even so, as has been seen, there are those who still suppose that the roots of Samaritanism

[41] Rowley, *The Samaritan Schism in Legend and History*, p. 210.

are in some sense to be traced to the events there described. More widespread, however, is the view that its origins are somehow to be related to the disasters that befell Judah in the sixth century, and in particular to the exile of many of her leading citizens to Babylon. On this view, it would be among those who remained in Palestine that we should look for the earliest Samaritans. We shall need first of all, then, to look at the evidence afforded by the great sixth-century prophets as to the state of affairs at this time; and then in the next section consider the period of restoration, and what we learn from Haggai and Zechariah.

Before considering the prophetic material more specifically, however, there are certain aspects of the background to this period which deserve attention. The broad outlines of the process by which Babylonian power was established in Palestine are well known, and need not be set out here.[42] Two points, however, are worth particular notice. The first is the fact that the deportations consequent upon the capture of Jerusalem in 597 and again in 587/6 were apparently not accompanied by the introduction of substantial numbers of settlers from other parts of the Babylonian Empire. The contrast with Assyrian policy at the time of the fall of Samaria is not as great as has sometimes been suggested, since we have seen that the picture of a single set of mass movements at that time is a misleading one. Nevertheless, there is a difference —whether because Babylonian practice in general was different, or because Judah was a remote and insignificant area, we cannot tell—and this difference was held to be of great significance when the later Jews came to reflect upon their history.

The second point of importance concerns the arrangements made by the Babylonians for the government of the newly-conquered areas. In general the Assyrian arrangements were maintained in the North,[43] but new arrangements were, of course, needed in Judah. The precise course of events is not entirely clear, but it would seem that after two experiments with Judahite representative rule had broken down, through the rebellion of the Davidide Zedekiah and the murder of Gedaliah who was not of royal blood but almost certainly a member of one of the established

[42] See the standard histories of Israel, by Noth or Bright, or Ackroyd, *Exile and Restoration.*
[43] Noth, *The Old Testament World* (London, 1966), p. 101.

ruling families (Jer. 40:6; cf. 26:24), no further locally-led or
-based administration was established. Judah then apparently
passed under the control of the provincial governor of Samaria—
a situation full of potential difficulties for the future.[44]

Our picture of the religious situation in Palestine after the fall
of Jerusalem is as fragmentary as our knowledge of the political
structure. The great prophets, from whom most of our knowledge
is derived, had other more basic concerns. One passage does,
however, command attention. We read in Jeremiah 41:5 that the
day after Gedaliah's murder, 'eighty men arrived from Shechem
and Shiloh and Samaria, with their beards shaved and their clothes
torn, and their bodies gashed, bringing cereal offerings and
incense to present at the temple of the LORD'. This group, it
may safely be assumed, was on its way to the site of the Jerusalem
temple,[45] the signs of mourning being an indication that the
Jerusalem cultus was no longer carried on, or, perhaps more
probably, a sign that it was being carried on in a reduced form
appropriate to its ruined condition.[46] Noth has argued that we
may see traces here of a regular custom of pilgrimage 'among the
descendants of the ancient tribes of Israel, in the former state of
Israel—at least in the province of Samaria, but probably even
beyond—to participate in the Jerusalem cult and to consider the
Jerusalem sanctuary as the official central sanctuary'.[47]

This passage in Jeremiah has been much discussed, and raises
a number of important points; but for our present purpose we
may note, first, that it gives a very clear indication of a continuing
veneration for Jerusalem in the great northern sanctuaries of
Shechem and Shiloh and in the administrative centre of Samaria,
and secondly, it suggests very strongly that some at least of the

[44] Alt, *Die Rolle Samarias bei der Entstehung des Judentums*, esp.
pp. 324–9.

[45] Despite the contrary argument of J. N. Schofield, *The Religious
Background of the Bible* (London, 1944), pp. 136f., who argues that the
pilgrims' destination was Mizpah.

[46] The point is discussed by D. R. Jones, 'The Cessation of Sacrifice
after the Destruction of the Temple in 586 B.C.', *JTS*, NS, xiv, 1963,
pp. 12–31, and by Ackroyd, *Israel under Babylon and Persia* (Oxford,
1970), p. 17.

[47] Noth, 'The Jerusalem Catastrophe of 587 B.C.', in *The Laws in
The Pentateuch and other Essays*, p. 264.

inhabitants of these places, far from being an alien and immigrant population as implied in 2 Kings 17, continued to look to Jerusalem as their religious centre. This very 'Deuteronomic' behaviour recorded in a section of the book of Jeremiah which has often been held to reflect Deuteronomic editing[48] might be regarded as historically suspect, but even if the story has been embellished, it shows that the northerners in general and the inhabitants of these cities in particular were not at this time viewed with disfavour. (It is just possible that the absence of any reference to pilgrims from Bethel might imply an unfavourable judgement on that sanctuary.[49])

There are no other comparably precise historical allusions in the prophetic material referring to this period, though the great sixth-century prophets—Jeremiah and Ezekiel particularly, Deutero-Isaiah less certainly—make reference to the inhabitants of the North. It is not practicable here to examine all such references and we must be content with the bald statement that there is no material in these prophetic works which can with any likelihood be considered as referring to the Samaritans in the sense in which later Judaism used that term.

Two types of reference are commonly found to which we may give brief attention. First, there are those passages which elaborate on the theme that the fate of Samaria was intended as a warning to Judah. This idea, already found in the comment upon the fall of Samaria in 2 Kings 17:18f., is also present in the eighth-century prophets, where in a number of passages the arrangement of the material shows that this is the basic point being established, whatever may be the critical judgement whether such passages should be taken as originating from the prophet to whom they are now ascribed. In the eight-century prophets examples of such passages are Isaiah 9:8 (M.T.: 9:7)–10:19 and possibly c. 28; Hosea 5; and Micah 1:5–9. The same point is also found on a smaller scale in single verses (e.g. Mic. 6:16). In Jeremiah and Ezekiel it is extremely common, and may range in scale from the remarkable verse in Jeremiah, 'Faithless Israel has shown herself less guilty than false Judah' (3:11), to the extended allegory of the two sisters, Oholah and Oholibah, in Ezekiel 23.

Secondly, both Jeremiah and Ezekiel contain many passages which look forward to a future restoration of the two kingdoms.

[48] So Nicholson, *Preaching to the Exiles.*    [49] Cf.Nielsen, *Shechem*, ch. 6.

This again is an established tradition, already found in earlier prophets (e.g. Hos. 1:10–2:1), and, though many such sections may be regarded as secondary, only *ex hypothesi* reasoning would reject them all. Basically, the point expressed is that the punishment inflicted by Yahweh upon the two kingdoms will not be permanent, and that they may hope for restoration. This would seem at once to exclude any suggestion that the faith of the northerners had been in any way permanently polluted through an admixture of pagan elements; rather, both communities were seen as having been punished and were now encouraged to look for better times. Such a section as Ezekiel 37:15–28 illustrates the nature of the expectation: the two sticks, for Ephraim and for Judah, will be joined, and Yahweh will 'make them one stick, that they may be one in my hand'. This theme of the restoration of both Judah and Ephraim is still found in Zechariah 10:6–12, a late passage, though its precise date is much disputed, and it is not until very much later that we find the picture of the 'ten lost tribes' set out in a way somewhat similar to the widely-held kind of belief outlined at the beginning of this study. 2 Esdras 13:40, which is probably not earlier than the Christian era, seems to be one of the earliest expressions of it.

There was therefore considerable fluidity in the thought of the great prophets of this period in relation to Northern Israel, in marked contrast to the hardening of attitudes which took place later. This is well illustrated by the 'booklet of consolation' for Ephraim in Jeremiah 30–1.[50] There the clear hope of the restoration of the northerners is expressed (30:3; 31:5, etc.) and no suggestion is made that developments had already taken place that would exclude such a possibility. The statement of G. von Rad that 30:1–3, is addressed 'to the exiles of the former Northern Kingdom'[51] may be too specific, but in any case he goes on to stress that the whole of Israel, North and South, was to share in the hoped-for salvation. It is noteworthy that Jeremiah 50:4 seems to imply that the exiles of both North and South were in Babylon (cf. also Jer. 50:17–20).

The total impression created by these and similar passages in

[50] The description is that of O. Eissfeldt, *The Old Testament: an Introduction* (Oxford, 1965), p. 361, based on Jer. 30:1–3.
[51] Von Rad, *Old Testament Theology*, II, p. 212.

both Jeremiah and Ezekiel is that analogies could properly be drawn between North and South. Just as their fate was similar because it had been brought about by similar sins on the part of the people, so they could equally look forward to restoration. And of course that restoration, when Yahweh brought it about, would be based on Jerusalem (at least for Jeremiah (31:6, etc.)—in Ezekiel, as we shall see, there is some dispute on this point) without any of the separatism which would be characteristic of Jews and Samaritans.

These general indications of attitude may suffice for our present consideration of Jeremiah, but the book of Ezekiel raises certain other problems, on account of the great diversity of critical attitudes which it has evoked. Thus, a number of scholars have held the view that Ezekiel was himself a northerner. James Smith regarded the prophet as originally having lived in the seventh century, in the time of Manasseh,[52] but others have argued for a northern origin while accepting the traditional dating. Thus, Gaster, in view of the geography underlying the temple-vision in the last chapters of Ezekiel, and of the fact that the Samaritans, usually so bitter against all Old Testament prophets, have nothing to say against Ezekiel, concludes that 'it looks as if he were of one of the Northern Tribes'.[53] None of the points used to support this theory of Ezekiel's northern origin is strong enough to overthrow the very clear testimony of every part of the book that Ezekiel's pressing concern was with Jerusalem, her fate, and the kind of future she might expect. Indeed, it is noteworthy that some scholars have found in Ezekiel not sympathy towards but polemic against the Samaritans; but this in turn has accompanied drastic critical emendation. It is associated in particular with the reconstruction of Judah's history put forward by C. C. Torrey, and will be considered below in that context. For the moment, however, we may recognize that the text of Ezekiel does present very considerable problems, but that these are best resolved by means of a process of expansion within an Ezekiel 'school', rather than by changing the date and place of the prophet himself. It will be assumed here that the prophet lived in the sixth century, and that the

[52] Jas. Smith, *The Book of the Prophet Ezekiel* (London, 1931), especially ch. 6.
[53] Gaster, *The Samaritans*, p. 15.

book incorporates much material that goes back to Ezekiel himself.

Disputes over the appropriate place of worship, with the rival claims of the temples on Mount Zion and Mount Gerizim, came to constitute a basic difference between Jews and Samaritans. It is therefore not surprising that the Temple-vision of Ezekiel 40–8 has been linked with arguments concerning Samaritanism. Here the disagreement among scholars concerning the amount of material which goes back to the prophet himself is particularly acute, but for our present purpose the first question at issue is the site of this ideal temple. It cannot simply be identified with the existing site on Mount Zion, and some scholars have therefore argued that a northern site, possibly linked with Shechem, is here implied. Thus C. Mackay, in a series of articles in the 1920s and 1930s, claimed that the basic point of these chapters was the rejection of Zion—which is never mentioned—from being the site of the temple of Yahweh. He regarded Shechem, the 'navel of the land', as its intended location, the 'very high mountain' of 40:2 being Mount Ebal, and the whole vision being understood as a kind of blueprint for the Samaritan Temple at Shechem.[54] A somewhat similar view is that of Gaster, who holds that Ezekiel 'rejects Jerusalem and selects a central spot in Palestine, which could be nothing else but Sichem or Mount Gerizim';[55] he also draws attention to the order in which the tribal allocations are set out in c. 48, an order which does not correspond with any other Old Testament list. Gaster claims that there is a remarkable similarity between the allocation here and that in the Samaritan Book of Joshua (Samaritan Chronicle IV on Macdonald's listing);[56] in fact when the claim is examined in detail the correspondence is much less close than Gaster alleges, and no weight can be put on this point.[57]

[54] C. Mackay, 'The Key of the Old Testament', *CQR*, 238, 1935, pp. 173–96. This article summarizes the viewpoints expressed by Mackay in a number of earlier articles.

[55] Gaster, *The Samaritans*, p. 15.      [56] Ibid., pp. 138f.

[57] Among other scholars who have supposed that the site of the Temple was to be associated with the Ebal-Gerizim complex is Smith (op. cit.); while L. E. Browne, *Ezekiel and Alexander* (London, 1952), p. 19, also sees the site of the Temple as being chosen with a view to uniting Judah and Samaria, though he is less specific about the location. (See also below, p. 113.)

In all this the negative arguments are a good deal more convincing than the positive. It is indeed likely that the site for the temple should not be precisely identified with Zion, yet it is certainly closely connected with it. It is widely held that Ezekiel had been familiar with Solomon's Temple, and perhaps had ministered in it;[58] the 'glory' theme in c. 43 and the frequent references to the Zadokite priesthood (40:46; 43:19, etc.) both suggest close links with Jerusalem, while the geography of c. 47, with the stream flowing down to the Arabah, also demands a southern location. (The Arabah is the Dead Sea or the region immediately south of it; Engedi is on the west bank of the Dead Sea; Eneglaim is unknown, but is usually taken to be in the same area, possibly near Ain Feschka or Qumran.[59]) All this suggests a location near, and possibly just to the north of, Zion; it is quite likely that, as in later apocalyptic writings, it would be wrong to try to locate the situation too exactly. Certainly the arrangement of the tribal areas in 47:13ff., though possibly linked with the P tradition of Numbers 34, seems in its present form to imply a complete breakaway from the original geographical and historical situation of the tribes, though the arrangement whereby seven tribes are placed north of the new Temple and five to the south may imply a recognition that Jerusalem was not in the true centre of the land but somewhat to the south.[60] The details of the arrangement of the tribes in chapters 47 and 48 seem to come from more than one period, so that, for example, Levi is sometimes included and sometimes not, while sometimes Joseph counts as one where elsewhere the division is made into two tribes, Ephraim and Manasseh. What is important is that here, as in chapters 36 and 37, the restoration of all the tribes of Israel is awaited.

For the most part, therefore, Ezekiel's picture of the situation is very similar to that of Jeremiah. In neither prophet is there any hint of a 'blotting-out' of the North after the fall of Samaria. In certain respects, however, Ezekiel goes further than Jeremiah,

[58] The point is fully discussed, with references to the views of other scholars, by Rowley, 'The Book of Ezekiel in Modern Study', in *Men of God*, pp. 204f.

[59] See W. R. Farmer, 'The Geography of Ezekiel's River of Life', in *The Biblical Archaeologist Reader*, 1 (New York, 1961), pp. 284–9.

[60] W. Eichrodt, *Ezekiel*, Old Testament Library (London, 1970), p. 593.

particularly in the way in which he stresses the racial impurity of the South. In particular, he will allow no claim to such purity on the part of Jerusalem: 'Your origin and your birth are of the land of the Canaanites; your father was an Amorite and your mother a Hittite' (16:3). In later Judaeo-Samaritan hostility considerations of this kind were to become of considerable importance.

One final point with regard to Ezekiel may be briefly noted. One of the arguments put forward by Smith in favour of Ezekiel's northern origin was his use of the word 'Israel', which he claims is here used to mean the Northern kingdom. (Smith cites 4:4–6 as a particularly clear example, but goes on to claim that similar usage can be found elsewhere.) Other more recent studies have shown that in fact no consistent pattern of usage can be found in Ezekiel. At times it means the exiled group; elsewhere the people of Judah and Jerusalem; elsewhere the people of the North; elsewhere again the whole people.[61] It is arbitrary to try to establish one precise usage as that which controls all the others. The point is significant, for this idea of the 'genuine' Israel was to become another important issue between Jews and Samaritans. Here in Ezekiel we appear to have reached a stage where the older pattern has broken up, but not yet one at which Israel becomes a more exclusively theological term, identified with the community centred upon Jerusalem.

Various points concerning Ezekiel will claim our attention again, but in the meanwhile it is appropriate to turn briefly to Deutero-Isaiah, since in Isaiah 40–8 especially the usage of 'Israel' is again noteworthy. Here it frequently denotes the community exiled from Judah to Babylon, often being used with 'Jacob' in synonymous parallelism. The limitation of the term is brought out very clearly by such a verse as 48:1:

> Hear this, O house of Jacob,
> who are called by the name of Israel,
> and who came forth from the loins [Heb: waters] of Judah.

This limitation of usage leads to the more general observation that there is apparently no reference at all to the Northern Israelites

---

[61] See J. Battersby Harford, *Studies in the Book of Ezekiel* (London, 1935), pp. 31ff., and G. A. Danell, *Studies in the Name Israel* (Uppsala, 1946), pp. 254ff.

throughout Isaiah 40–55. There is, indeed, only one aspect of these chapters that need concern us here. There has been much argument in recent years whether or not it is proper to speak of Deutero-Isaiah as a 'universalist'.[62] Without entering into this dispute, we may at least note that if universalism may properly be spoken of, it has certain very definite presuppositions accompanying it. Deutero-Isaiah, like the other prophets of the sixth century, knew and alluded to a wide variety of sacral traditions in his people's history—Abraham, Jacob, the Exodus, Zion— yet his theological application of them is confined to the community exiled in Babylon. In this he is narrower than Ezekiel, where a more general restoration is envisaged. It is often maintained that Deutero-Isaiah's vision was a larger one than that of Ezekiel, but found little response in post-exilic Judaism; in this respect the reverse is true, and it was the more limited view of Deutero-Isaiah, applying the promises to those in Babylon, which came to prevail. The status both of the northerners and of those who had remained in Judah during the exile came thus to be lowered. Indeed, as we shall see, these two groups came to be identified with one another, and both would be dismissed as no part of the true people of God.

## The Period of Restoration

The identification mentioned at the end of the previous section, between the northerners and those who remained in Judah during the time when others were exiled to Babylon, is not really made explicit in the Old Testament itself, and is first clearly traceable in Josephus, whose reconstruction of the history of his people will be considered in a later section. Even so, a number of modern scholars have accepted such an identification, either deliberately or by implication, and have then described this amalgam as

[62] Objections to the usual view have been raised from quite different standpoints by P. A. H. de Boer, *Second Isaiah's Message* (Leiden, 1956), pp. 8off.; by N. H. Snaith, in H. M. Orlinsky and N. H. Snaith, 'Studies on the Second Part of the Book of Isaiah', *VTS*, 14 (Leiden, 1967), pp. 154ff.; and by I. Engnell, 'The Messiah in the Old Testament and Judaism', in *Critical Essays on the Old Testament* (London, 1970), pp. 215ff.

Samaritan. Thus R. S. Foster interprets all the disputes referred to in the prophets of this period in 'Jew v. Samaritan' terms and assumes that the basis of controversy between the two groups was to be found in these years of restoration: 'The dispute began in the early days of the Return, although it did not reach its culmination until the days of Nehemiah and Ezra when the breach between Jew and Samaritan became final.'[63] As will shortly become apparent, other scholars have taken a broadly similar line. It will be seen, therefore, that we are now considering a period when it is widely held that Samaritanism can properly be spoken of as a rival to the Judaism of Jerusalem. Whereas it is generally agreed that no reference to Samaritanism can be found among the great sixth-century prophets—unless their sixth-century dating be denied—it is not possible to claim any comparable measure of agreement with regard to the prophetic writings from the last part of the sixth century, or with regard to the historical events to which they make allusion.

Of this prophetic material—Isaiah 56–66, Haggai and Zechariah 1–8—it is appropriate to examine Isaiah 56–66 first, not only because it stands somewhat apart from the other literature concerned, but also because of its links with the earlier parts of the Isaiah collection. As to the nature of that relation, there is still no agreement, and indeed most aspects of the literary and historical background of these chapters remain in dispute. Some scholars have seen them as forming an integral whole with chapters 40–55, others as coming from disciples of Deutero-Isaiah, others again as being an independent collection of oracles from a variety of sources.[64] There is, however, some measure of agreement on a late sixth-century dating and a Palestinian milieu as providing the most likely setting for these chapters, and that view will be followed here, without any attempt to make judgements upon the literary problems. Certainly if there is a Palestinian background, the possibility of these chapters being relevant to Samaritanism would be so much the greater. To be more precise is not possible.

[63] R. S. Foster, *The Restoration of Israel* (London, 1970), p. 117.

[64] No attempt is here made to spell out these different approaches in detail, the intention being simply to note the variety of ways in which these chapters have been understood. For fuller documentation, see the various critical introductions to the Old Testament.

We may only say that if the chapters come from a single hand, the frequency of references to Jerusalem and Judah might suggest that as their area of origin, whereas, if a greater diversity is seen here, it is not in itself impossible that some sections may have a northern background.

Three separate sections in these chapters have in fact been considered to refer to Judaeo-Samaritan divisions: 56:9–57:13; 63:7–64:11; and 65 and 66 (taking these two chapters as closely related to one another, even though in their present form there are diverse elements within them). Before considering these passages more closely, it is important to remember that the presence of 'Samaritan' elements within them has usually been taken to imply, either that a racially impure community already existed in the North, in accordance with the older understanding of 2 Kings 17, or that these chapters should be given a very late dating and that they contain allusions to historical events about which we should otherwise know nothing. Either of these assumptions involves considerable difficulties, and consequently the majority of recent commentators find no Samaritan reference here, and prefer to explain the sections mentioned in terms of internal dissensions within the Jerusalem community after the return of some of its members from exile and in the face of the problems of re-establishing their cultic and economic life.

The first of these passages is 56:9–57:13, which was first understood in this way by B. Duhm, who was followed, with reservations, by J. Skinner.[65] The violent condemnations of idolatrous practice in c. 57 were commonly held among earlier critics to be a pre-exilic oracle which had been reinterpreted and reapplied to the later situation. Duhm argued that those here condemned were the Samaritans; Skinner allowed 'some plausibility' to the suggestion, but finally concluded that a more probable explanation of this section was that it was aimed at 'a paganized Judaean population, closely akin to the Samaritans of the North, and cultivating friendly relations with them'.[66] Skinner went on in his more detailed commentary to note that certain difficulties

[65] B. Duhm, *Das Buch Jesaja* (4th edition, Göttingen, 1922; originally published in 1892); J. Skinner, *Isaiah XL–LXVI*, Cambridge Bible, (Cambridge, 1910).
[66] Op. cit., p. 154.

were raised for the 'Samaritan' view by 57:11, with its apparently more conciliatory note.

There are, however, more basic objections than this extremely ambiguous verse to be raised against the 'Samaritan' interpretation. The first is that to connect this passage with the Samaritans seems to be entirely gratuitous. Nothing of what is here condemned is associated in any way with known Samaritan practice, save in Jewish polemic at an age when all idolatrous practices came quite unjustly to be associated with the Samaritans. There is also a methodological objection, which applies here and to a number of other similar prophetic passages which we shall have to consider. No doubt some particular events inspired this oracle, but it is a very perilous procedure to attempt to work back to the historical situation from the end-product in the prophetic collection. During the second world war in this country there were from time to time 'national days of prayer'. If one came across the form of service used on such an occasion, one might well deduce that some military or other disaster had taken place, but it would be rash to attempt to work out in detail what it was. Similarly, the application of form-critical methods should warn us that the widespread use of particular literary types will probably preclude us from being able to associate specific passages with specific historical circumstances. Not surprisingly, therefore, more recent commentators on these chapters seem to have abandoned the attempt to pin down exactly either the historical situation or the precise identity of those condemned,[67] while one writer has reverted to the hypothesis of the re-use of earlier material.[68] We must therefore be content to remain uncertain whether the reference in the passage is to the past sins of Zion which had led to the Exile, or to her present falling-away. In either case, the natural reference is to Jerusalem and her community, and whenever the passage is dated, no Samaritan reference seems likely.

With the other passages under consideration a similar difference in emphasis may be noted between the commentaries of a generation or more ago and more recent writers. The older tendency was to find specific historical allusions in the passage being discussed,

[67] So e.g. J. Muilenburg, in IB, V (New York, 1956), pp. 660ff.
[68] C. Westermann, *Isaiah 40-66*, Old Testament Library (London, 1969), pp. 301f.

and if none were forthcoming, there was the temptation to construct a situation that would fit all the given requirements. This is very characteristic of the treatment of these chapters by L. E. Browne, whose *Early Judaism* is perhaps the most thoroughgoing exposition of the 'Samaritan' view. (The copy I have been using has been marked by its former owner, Professor W. O. E. Oesterley, at the chapter, 'The Rejected Samaritans', with the comment, 'Not convincing though ingenious'. Dr. Oesterley's judgement seems a sound one.) Thus the usual modern view is to take 63:7–64:11 as a unit whose literary form is that of the psalm of lamentation, rather than to divide it into a number of sections. On this view it 'is undatable with any precision because of the general nature of its allusions. To interpret particular statements— as for example here the problematic Abraham reference of 63:16— as precise allusions to specific historic conditions is hazardous'.[69] Ackroyd's approach, here quoted, is that which is now usual, and is in marked contrast with the attempt to delineate here a situation in which the speaker is a Samaritan prophet (Browne entitles his treatment of this section, 'The Plaint of a Samaritan Prophet'),[70] bewailing both the sin of his people and the fact that they are now being excluded by the Judahites from the community of Israel. In this situation of dereliction, appeal is being made to God for restoration and justice.

The particular crux within this section is 63:15–19, and especially v. 16, where the exact force of $y^e d\bar{a}'\bar{a}nu$ (EVV: know us) is disputed, and it is unclear whether the references to Abraham and Israel are to the patriarchs as individuals or to the contemporary nation. In the following verse 'the tribes of thy heritage' is a phrase that has been differently interpreted, and similarly 'thy holy cities' of 64:10. (Here the singular 'holy city' of LXX and Vulgate looks like an emendation to bring the phrase into line with Zion and Jerusalem in the remainder of the verse.) Again, on an 'historical' understanding of this section, problems are raised by 63:18f. and numerous emendations have been suggested.[71] But to a large extent these difficulties are self-created; if the language is that traditional to the psalm of lament, with a heavy

[69] Ackroyd, *Exile and Restoration*, pp. 227f.
[70] *Early Judaism* (Cambridge, 1929), pp. 70–86.
[71] See Browne, op. cit., pp. 76ff.; Foster, op. cit., pp. 114–17.

dependence upon stereotyped phrases appropriate in general
rather than with particular reference, there is no need to emend
the text in order to discover historical precision.

On three grounds, therefore, it seems as if the 'Samaritan'
interpretation of this section is unsatisfactory. First, as has already
been noted, the formal structure of the passage leads us to suppose
that we have here to do with a psalm of lament, of the kind found
both in the canonical Psalter and in Lamentations. As such, the
textual difficulties largely disappear, in that the attempt to provide
precise points of reference for doubtful words and phrases is
avoided. Secondly, if such a passage really did originate from a
Samaritan prophet, and can be recognized in this way by modern
scholars, it seems remarkable that those responsible for creating
the book of Isaiah in its present form failed to see it as such, and
came to incorporate it into their own sacred traditions. The force
of this objection was recognized by A. Guillaume, who otherwise
accepted Browne's view, and he answered it by saying that 'the
schism had not yet occurred'.[72] This may indeed be true, but it at
once removes the main grounds for suggesting Samaritanism here
in the first place—the sense of division and bitterness which seem
to underlie this passage. Thirdly, and leading out of this last point,
the 'Samaritan' interpretation can only have any weight if there
was already existing a state of hostility between the two communities. This would mean either accepting the traditional undertaking
of 2 Kings 17, or making this passage an extremely late addition
to the book of Isaiah. Neither of these assumptions seems to be
either necessary or justifiable.

Finally, in our consideration of Isaiah 56–66, some examination
is required of chapters 65 and 66, which have been related to
Samaritanism in two distinct ways. First, as might be anticipated,
Browne links this section also with the Samaritans. He regards
these chapters as being 'in some respects an answer to the Samaritan Plaint of lxiii. 7–lxiv'.[73] In 65 the problem is to identify those
whose religious practices are being referred to. It is common
ground that some part of Israel rather than any foreign nation is
alluded to, and the usual opinion now is that the practices referred

[72] A. Guillaume, *Isaiah XL–LXVI*, in *A New Commentary on Holy
Scripture* (London, 1951 ( =26) ), p. 1481.

[73] Op. cit., p. 94.

to in vv. 1–16 can best be explained as taking place within the community directly addressed by the prophet, that is, presumably, the Jews at Jerusalem. Browne, however, takes the references here as a condemnation of the heathen practices into which the Samaritans had fallen, together with an assurance of Yahweh's continuing concern for them. The opening verses of c. 66 are seen as a warning against the dangers inherent in temple-worship, with v. 5 understood as a word of comfort to those Samaritans who had mourned over Jerusalem in her downfall. (Psalm 80, often noted as showing Northern Israelite characteristics, is cited as stemming from a similar background, though Browne himself acknowledges the risks inherent in the attempt to pin down individual Psalms to particular historical situations,[74] and this point would be even more strongly stressed by most contemporary students of the Psalter.)

The objections to this treatment of these chapters are basically the same as those already noted in regard to the earlier section, with the further point that it is even clearer here that the divisions referred to are divisions within the Jewish community itself. 65:8–12 brings this out with particular force. It must also be borne in mind that the abuses here condemned have no connection with what is known of Samaritan practice; some form of apostasy seems to be implied, in a way not unlike the condemnations of Ezekiel 8, where also malpractices within Judah were being attacked.

It would appear therefore, that no direct link with Samaritanism is to be found in this section. Indirectly, however, it is possible that these chapters furnish important clues concerning Samaritan origins. It has often been noted that we find here the development, already implicit in Ezekiel, but now much more marked, according to which divisions exist within Israel; the blessing and the curse are to be given to specific groups within the one community. Thus C. Westermann, commenting on 66:5, notes that it 'presumes that signs of a cleavage were beginning to appear in Judah in the early post-Exilic period. . . . So far, however, the cleavage had not led to the formation of different parties.'[75] Later, such a cleavage

[74] Op. cit., p. 105.
[75] Op. cit., pp. 416f. A similar judgement is expressed in more general terms by W. Harrelson, *Interpreting the Old Testament* (New York, 1964), p. 251.

would assume the form of distinct parties—a state of affairs which becomes significant for our present examination, since Samaritanism takes on its distinctive characteristics precisely at that point when the formation of such groups had become a very characteristic feature of Judaism.

Before leaving the consideration of Isaiah 65–6, there is a different type of connection with Samaritanism which has been suggested and which must briefly be considered here. In 66:1f., the reference to temple-building has often been understood by commentators as aimed against the building of the Temple on Mount Gerizim by the Samaritans. Here, as so often with the book of Isaiah, the suggestion seems to have originated with Duhm,[76] and was followed by a number of the older commentators. Thus G. W. Wade argued that the reference was not to a rebuilding of the Temple on Mount Zion, but was aimed 'against the design, entertained by the adversaries of the loyal section of the Jews, of erecting a second, and rival sanctuary. Such a design, which was eventually carried out by the Samaritans on Mount Gerizim, was illegitimate according to the Deuteronomic law.'[77] It will be observed that Wade does not specifically state that there is a direct reference here to the intention of building a temple on Mount Gerizim, though if that is not his purpose, it is difficult to see why the comparison should have been made. In any case, the actual terms of the denunciation would not then be very appropriate; there is no possible allusion to the Deuteronomic law, and it is not so much a particular project as any temple building which is here denounced. Similarly Skinner, though he also favours the Gerizim interpretation, goes on to admit that 'if the erection of a schismatic Temple were referred to, we should have expected a much more explicit and vigorous condemnation of the project'.[78] This difficulty, coupled with the absence of any suggestion that the Samaritans considered building their own temple before the fourth century, suffices to make the whole line of interpretation an improbable one. Much more naturally, this passage might be linked with those other Old Testament passages which stress the

[76] Op. cit., pp. 481f.
[77] G. W. Wade, *The Book of the Prophet Isaiah*, Westminster Commentary (London, 1929 ( = 11) ), p. 414.
[78] Op. cit., p. 223.

heavenly dwelling of Yahweh and are cautious about some of the cruder implications of his earthly worship (cf. in particular the contrast drawn in 1 Kings 8 between Yahweh's earthly and his heavenly dwelling, the warning of Jeremiah in his 'temple-speech', Jer. 7, and Ps. 50). Finally, the force of the interrogative in 66:1, *'ēy-zeh*, would be 'where?' or 'what kind of?'—both usages can be paralleled elsewhere in the Old Testament[79]—it seems to be most naturally taken in a theological rather than a geographical or historical sense.

Such an understanding of the passage would also tell against the argument of J. D. Smart, that it should be associated with the building of the second Temple in Jerusalem, and seen as a contrast to the attitude of Haggai and Zechariah, with their enthusiastic support for that project.[80] Smart's view has been developed and made more precise by Foster, who recognizes that insuperable difficulties are raised by associating this passage with any temple other than that in Jerusalem, and suggests that this section is aimed against 'not the temple building *as such, but what it has in fact become*, namely a source of bitterness, narrowness and separation'.[81] He goes on to suggest that 66:5 is addressed to the Samaritans, for whom 7–9 represent an oracle of hope. Once again, we are left with the feeling that this is an ingenious but over-precise attribution of what are admittedly difficult passages; and that it is remarkable how the true significance of this section has apparently escaped not only two thousand years of scholarship, but also the compilers of the book of Isaiah, who certainly did not understand these passages in such a way.[82]

It has been necessary when considering Isaiah 56–66 to refer to a number of older—some might say outdated—commentaries. Two points arising from this may be noted. The first is simply that, as has been indicated, the general tenor of more recent commentaries is to avoid precise historical identification, both because

[79] Skinner, op. cit., p. 221, argued in favour of the rendering 'what manner of?' but most recent commentators have been content with the translation 'where?'. See the discussion in Muilenburg, IB, V, pp. 757–60.

[80] J. D. Smart, *History and Theology in Second Isaiah* (London, 1967), pp. 281ff.

[81] Op. cit., p. 112. (Italics in original.)

[82] For a different approach to these chapters, which is not of direct relevance to the present study, see Westermann, op. cit., pp. 411ff.

of our lack of knowledge of the history, and also because of a recognition that many of the literary forms used imply a stereotyping and a generalization which make historical certainty impossible. But that does not imply that reference to the older commentators is now unncessary, for the second point is that many of the historical treatments of this period still attempt to use these and other prophetic passages in this older way. Beside the immediate consideration of Samaritan origins, therefore, it may be that a greater readiness to admit the severe limitations of our historical knowledge is also needed.

Such considerations apply with particular force to Isaiah 56–66, where not only the general consideration mentioned above, but also the peculiar difficulties concerning the understanding of these chapters which have already been noted, must be borne in mind. 'The uncertainties in discovering appropriate backgrounds for the material in [Isaiah] 56–66 are such that it is here particularly easy to fall into the trap of dating the material in order to discover evidence about the period to which it has been assigned', is Ackroyd's apt warning.[83] Even when we feel that an identifiable historical situation does underlie a particular section, the question of possible Samaritan reference still remains.

If we now turn from Isaiah 56–66 to Haggai, at least one of these problems is less acute, for it is generally agreed that the dates given, though they may form part of the editorial framework of the book rather than represent the original words of the prophet himself, nevertheless are substantially reliable. With Haggai, that is to say, unlike Isaiah 56–66, we can assume with fair confidence that we know something of the background and circumstances of his prophecy. Moreover, these circumstances were such as to add particular point to our examination of Haggai. We have already noted that it is a widely-held view that the real roots of Samaritanism are to be found in the changed circumstances of sixth-century Palestine, and the upheaval brought about by the Babylonian exile. On this view it was the tension between those who had been in exile and those who had never left Palestine which provides the first evidence of Samaritanism, and Haggai is of particular importance precisely because his prophecies were directed to one such area of tension. As has been indicated, the suggestion that

[83] *Exile and Restoration*, p. 119.

Samaritan allusions should be found in the material so far considered is confined to a minority of scholars and represents a somewhat old-fashioned view; by contrast, the idea that a schism took place in the sixth century and is first traceable in Haggai is a view which has won wide support ever since it was first set out in 1908 by J. W. Rothstein.[84]

It would seem that there are four questions raised by the book of Haggai which concern our present purpose. First, what do we learn of the state of the Temple and its rebuilding, and how does this evidence relate to that of the early chapters of Ezra? Secondly, what is the force of the terms 'people of the land' (2:4) and 'this people' (2:14), and is there any relation with the usage in Ezra 4:4? Thirdly, is it legitimate to understand 2:10–14 as addressed not to the Jerusalem community but to the Samaritans, either originally, or by a later reinterpretation? Finally, in more general terms, does Haggai offer any evidence concerning the political separation of Judah from Samaria within the Persian imperial system—an issue which became of considerable significance in the following century, and might be thought to have its roots at this time? These four questions will be considered in turn.

First, then, the question of the rebuilding of the Temple. The prima facie impression created by the book is that at the time of Haggai's appeal to the people nothing had been done towards rebuilding. 'Is it a time for yourselves to dwell in panelled houses, while this house lies in ruins?' (1:4). It is not necessary here to enter into the discussion of what exactly is meant by 'panelled' (*sᵉpūnīm*)—clearly a contrast is being made between comparative comfort and the ruined state (*ḥārēb*) of the Temple. *Ḥārēb* usually implies desolation, and the most natural understanding of this would be that nothing of any consequence had yet been done to restore the damage inflicted by Nebuchadnezzar's army. The statement in Ezra 3:10–13, which implies that the foundations of the Temple had been laid some years earlier, is not entirely irreconcilable with this, so that, for example, *ḥārēb* may have the general sense of desertion and neglect rather than a more precise and limited statement that nothing had been done to the building.[85]

[84] J. W. Rothstein, 'Juden und Samaritaner', *BWAT*, 3 (Leipzig, 1908).
[85] So F. I. Andersen, 'Who built the Second Temple?', *ABR*, VI, 1958, pp. 1–35.

Some scholars, therefore, accept the substantial accuracy of the account in Ezra 3. Thus, for example, Ackroyd accepts that 'the first period of the return would seem to be marked by a rather ineffective attempt at restoration',[86] and that it was because this initial impulse petered out that the reproaches of Haggai were necessary. Others, however, have seen the story in Ezra 3 as an idealized account, 'what must have happened', rather than as historical, and to those who take this view it was the urging of Haggai and Zechariah which was necessary before any work was done on the Temple. Thus D. Winton Thomas states categorically: 'The writings of these two prophets make it certain that the rebuilding was only begun in 520.'[87]

Just as some uncertainty exists as to the precise force of $\hbar\bar{a}r\bar{e}b$, so a similar problem arises with $y\bar{a}sad$, the word used in Haggai 2:18 and in Ezra 3:10–12, and usually translated in the sense of laying a foundation stone. Both F. I. Andersen[88] and A. Gelston[89] have argued that the word has a greater range of meaning than the modern sense of laying a foundation. Its force can be primarily religious rather than constructional, and the passage in Haggai need not preclude some kind of start having been made a number of years previously. Here again, therefore, there is some uncertainty, with different interpretations of the statements in Ezra being possible—a fact which it will be necessary to bear in mind when the early chapters of Ezra are considered more fully.

Our first question has been of a general kind, trying to establish something of the circumstances of Haggai's work. The second question is more directly related to the Samaritan issue. It concerns the use of the phrase '*am hā'āreṣ* (people of the land) in 2:4, and the other phrases that seem to be related to it. The question involves us first of all in clarifying our picture of the arrangement of the material in the book. The traditional view of the composition of Haggai, that it consists of four oracles delivered within a period

[86] *Exile and Restoration*, p. 144.

[87] D. Winton Thomas in IB, VI (New York, 1956), p. 1038. The problem is fully discussed by K. Galling, 'Serubbabel und der Hohepriester bei Wiederaufbau des Tempels in Jerusalem', in *Studien zur Geschichtę Israels im persischen Zeitalter* (Tübingen, 1964), pp. 127–48 esp. pp. 132–4.        [88] Art. cit.

[89] A. Gelston, 'The Foundations of the Second Temple', *VT*, XVI 2, 1966, pp. 232–5.

of five months *c.* 520 B.C. and then incorporated into a book, probably by the prophet himself, is now widely questioned. The oracles themselves may no doubt be accepted as genuine products of that period, but questions are raised with regard to the purpose and circumstances of their composition, and the presence of later editorial work. Particularly important in this respect is the study of W. A. M. Beuken, who argues convincingly that the book in its present form was edited by a group associated with the work of the Chronicler.[90]

Bearing this in mind we can now ask just what force should be ascribed to the various phrases used in the description of different groups within the community. The phrase most frequently found as a description of the returned exiles is *šeʾērīt hāʿām* (Hagg. 1:12, 14; 2:2; cf. Zech. 8:11f.); apparently a deliberate contrast is being drawn between the group so designated and those who had remained in Palestine. (A similar idea may be found at Isaiah 46:3 and—though not with the same phraseology—at 2 Chronicles 36:20 and Ezra 4:1-5.) The Ezra passage, indeed, is concerned with the same period as Haggai, but since it forms part of the Chronicler's presentation of this period in terms of the restoration of the true people of God to their inheritance, it seems best to defer the consideration of that section of Ezra until it can be seen in the context of the whole of the Chronicler's presentation.

To return to Haggai; the fact that *šeʾērīt*[91] *hāʿām* is frequently found as a description of the community led to the suggestion found in older critical editions of the Hebrew Bible,[92] that the same phrase should be read here in place of *ʿam hāʾāreṣ*. This view —which has been abandoned in more recent editions[93]—was criticized, as being arbitrary and without versional support, by Nicholson, who went on to argue that, though *ʿam hāʾāreṣ* was the right reading here, it should not be supposed that the term had any fixed and rigid usage in the Old Testament.[94] There is

[90] W. A. M. Beuken, 'Haggai-Sacharja 1–8', *Studia Semitica Neerlandica*, 10 (Assen, 1967).

[91] See section, 'Ezra and the Chronicler' below, esp. pp. 64–7.

[92] O. Procksch, in R. Kittel, *Biblia Hebraica*, 3rd ed., 1933, and reprints.

[93] K. Elliger, in *Biblia Hebraica Stuttgartensia*, 1970. The whole phrase is, however, still noted as a possible addition.

[94] Nicholson, 'The Meaning of the Expression עַם הָאָרֶץ in the Old Testament', *JSS*, X 1, 1965, pp. 59–66.

obviously a danger in attempting to be too precise, but, despite Nicholson's warnings, there still seems to be some validity in the older suggestion that the use of such a phrase specifically indicated a social grouping which might be defined as a 'clearly defined stratum of the free Yahwistic society'.[95] If such an understanding is correct, it would make good sense when applied to this passage, in the context of encouragement by the prophet to help in the restoration of former glories. Alternatively, Ackroyd has suggested that *'am hā'āreṣ* is the phrase original to Haggai, and that it was modified by the compilers because of the derogatory implications that it subsequently came to have.[96] If this is so, there would be no significant difference in meaning here between *'am hā'āreṣ* and *šeʿērīṭ hāʿām*.

On either of these last interpretations, the important point for our present purpose is that there is no reference here to the Samaritans. Haggai's message was essentially addressed to the people of Judah and Jerusalem, and it was their shortcomings against which he aimed his denunciations. By such an interpretation, our third question, concerning 2:10–14, is already partially answered. The view taken by many commentators would then be appropriate, that this passage is addressed to the same group as are the other oracles in the book, and is occasioned by a further failure to live up to the prophet's—and his God's—expectations.[97]

Another view of this section has, however, been widely held. Many commentators and interpreters of the history of this period have followed the suggestion originally made by Rothstein that the reference to 'this people' in 2:14 is aimed against the Samaritans.[98] This view is largely based on the sharp difference in tone between

[95] E. Würthwein, 'Der "Am Ha'arez im Alten Testament", *BWANT*, 4e Folge, Heft 17, 1936.

[96] Ackroyd, *Exile and Restoration*, p. 162.

[97] This view was already set out by H. G. Mitchell, in Mitchell, J. M. P. Smith and H. G. Bewer, *Haggai, Zechariah, Malachi and Jonah*, ICC (Edinburgh, 1912), pp. 67–9, and has returned to favour after a period when the suggestion noted in the following paragraph was more generally accepted.

[98] So among commentators Elliger, *Buch der 12 kleinen Propheten*, II, ATD, (Göttingen, 4th ed., 1959), p. 91; D. Winton Thomas, IB, V, p. 1047; and many other writers, of whom K. Koch 'Haggais unreines Volk', *ZAW*, 79, 1967, pp. 55f., lists eleven.

this section and the word of encouragement which has immediately preceded it. But this difficulty only arises because of the dates which play so prominent a part in Haggai, and, as Beuken has shown, these may well be the contribution of the final compilers. Furthermore the juxtaposing of words of encouragement and of doom is a common enough feature in the prophetic collections.[99] Even if a Samaritan interpretation were to be accepted, and this passage closely linked with a similar understanding of Ezra 4:1ff., it is important to note that there is nothing here of the later charges of racial impurity which Jews brought against Samaritans. This is stressed by Browne, who likens the attack here to 'the old tribal jealousy between the North and South kingdoms',[100] thereby introducing into Haggai's words—quite gratuitously—the assumption that those here addressed were northerners or the descendants of such. Many comments on supposed Samaritan references share this ambiguity, seeing the Samaritans now as descendants of the old Northern kingdom, now as alien immigrants. Browne further suggested that the difference between the priestly answer here concerning the contagious effects of holiness and the statements in the law concerning sin-offerings (Lev. 6:27f.) was prompted by the anxiety to prevent holiness being imparted to the Samaritans; but Old Testament texts from different traditions rarely achieve the degree of consistency that this implies.[101]

Such speculation, though ingenious, seems quite unnecessary. Much more natural than the interpretation which regards these verses as aimed against Samaritans—in whatever sense that term be understood—is to suppose that 'this people' here, as in 1:2, refers to the same community as all the surrounding passages. Other suggestions seem, as Ackroyd notes, 'to have been dictated by a too close adherence to the chronological order of Haggai's prophecies as indicated by the present form of the Massoretic text'.[102] Ackroyd has, however, made a further suggestion, the

[99] Beuken, op. cit., pp. 21ff.; Ackroyd, *Exile and Restoration*, pp. 166f.
[100] Browne, op. cit., pp. 61f.
[101] Op. cit., pp. 109–12; cf. Snaith, *Distinctive Ideas of the Old Testament* (London, 1944), p. 42.
[102] Ackroyd, *Exile and Restoration*, p. 166. Similar conclusions are reached—though by different methods—by H. G. May, ' "This People" and "This Nation" in Haggai', *VT*, XVIII, 1968, pp. 190–7; and Koch, art. cit., pp. 52–66.

acceptability of which must to some extent be governed by the view taken of the Chronicler's purpose. For the moment, then, we may note it without attempting to reach a decision on it. The suggestion is that this section may have been reinterpreted from its original context to refer to the Samaritans when the book was finally put into its present form, probably in the milieu associated with the Chronicler. On this view it would be in that context that this oracle was used 'to prove that God had rejected as unclean the worship and life of another community, the Samaritans'.[103]

It would seem, therefore, that the attempt to establish the fact of an already existing division between the Jerusalem Jews and the Samaritans on the basis of the oracles of Haggai cannot be sustained. It remains to ask our last question: does Haggai offer any evidence concerning the political relationship of Judah and Samaria within the Persian Empire? It is noteworthy that Zerub-babel is referred to as 'governor' (*peḥāh*) of Judah (1:1, etc.), and the same title is used of Nehemiah (Neh. 5:14), of the other governors of the Persian province 'Beyond-the-River' (Neh. 2:7, etc.), and also of Sheshbazzar in the Aramaic section of Ezra (Ezra 5:14). If we follow the commonly-held view that the book of Malachi should be dated in the first half of the fifth century between the time of Haggai and that of Nehemiah then the reference to 'the governor' at Malachi 1:8 may also be noted here.

Our knowledge is too fragmentary to dispel the extremely allusive character of these references, and two lines of interpretation at least may be regarded as consonant with the evidence. It may be that the apparently once-for-all nature of Nehemiah's mission is the somewhat misleading impression created by the memorialist who wished to emphasize the importance of Nehemiah's role, and that he was in fact one of a series of Persian representatives in Jerusalem, a line reaching back to Sheshbazzar and Zerubbabel. In this case Malachi 1:8 would fit quite naturally into the context, further support would be given by Nehemiah's reference to 'the former governors who were before me' (Neh. 5:15), and it is even possible that a list of these men is to be found in Ezra 2:2 (= Neh. 7:7), where several of the names, here presented as if they were

---

[103] Ackroyd, 'Studies in the Book of Haggai', *JJS*, 2, 1951, pp. 163–76; 3, 1952, pp. 1–13; 3, p. 3. Cf. also his article 'Haggai', in *The New Peake Commentary* (London, 1962), pp. 644f.

contemporaries of one another, are in fact those of known governors. But it is equally possible that such a reconstruction is too precise. We might feel that the word *peḥāh* (which a recent lexicon describes as 'a rather vague title')[104] could more appropriately be translated 'commissioner', and that the missions of Sheshbazzar, Zerubbabel and Nehemiah were basically *ad hoc* authorizations to carry out a specific task. In this case both Malachi 1:8 and Nehemiah 5:15 would be understood as references to the governor in Samaria. This view is that of Alt, who held that no final establishment of a governorship in Jerusalem took place before the time of Nehemiah, and that previously Jerusalem had been in a somewhat anomalous position, since Samaria had been within the imperial system since Assyrian times, whereas the assignment of special administrators to Jerusalem was a new development.[105]

There appears to be no evidence from the Persian side which would help towards a decision between these alternative reconstructions, and it is probably best to leave the question open. In either case the basic cause of tension between North and South at this period would centre on the claims of the imperial authorities in Samaria, rather than the mass of the people. Indeed, Alt suggested that much of the friction may have been related to what we should call 'administrative' matters, such as questions concerning landed property which the earlier imperial regime had confiscated, rather than the more 'religious' concerns upon which the biblical narrative concentrates.

This leads us on to a further reason for scepticism in the face of any alleged Samaritan reference in Haggai. The book, as we have seen, is most unlikely to have contained any reference to northerners. In the treatment of the events of this period in Ezra 4, written perhaps 150–200 years later, veiled and somewhat obscure allusions to northerners of a somewhat derogatory kind are being made. By the time of Josephus, in the first century A.D., the identification of the opposition to the Jerusalem Jews with the Samaritans is clear and unequivocal (Josephus, *Ant.*, XI, 96f.). What is curious is the fashion in which many modern

[104] W. L. Holladay, *A Concise Hebrew and Aramaic Lexicon of the Old Testament* (Leiden, 1971), p. 291.
[105] Alt, *Die Rolle Samarias bei der Entstehung des Judentums*, esp. pp. 331ff.

scholars have in effect followed the latest rather than the earliest testimony in their reconstruction of these events. Thus, for example, Murphy, whose caution in regard to 2 Kings 17 was noted earlier, is here by contrast quite willing to accept this much later testimony: the especial problem for the Jerusalem community at this time, he writes, was 'the hostility of its neighbours *in Samaria*. . . . The seed was sown for the classical enmity between Jews and Samaritans.'[106] No biblical account mentions Samaria at this point.

The silence of Haggai with regard to the North is equally characteristic of Zechariah 1–8 (the only part of the book which is usually reckoned to have any direct connection with the prophet after whom it is named). Only in the textually very dubious 7:2 might a possible northern reference be found. Some commentators do not regard the word 'Bethel' here as a reference to the place of that name at all, at least as the text originally stood,[107] but even if such an identification was original, there is still no reference to Shechem or to Samaria. For this reason, the conclusion reached by Winton Thomas in regard to this passage seems unsatisfactory, for he maintains that, as with Haggai 2:10ff., this passage shows 'the same unfriendly attitude to the Northern—Samaritan— population'.[108] But since, as we have already noted, hostility toward Bethel was of long standing in Jerusalemite circles, there seems no need to bring in a Samaritan reference to explain this.

Very characteristic of the imprecision with which the term 'Samaritan' is used is Foster's treatment of this verse, where, after reaching the conclusion that the reference to the place Bethel was original, he then adds: 'Bethel, now, was one of the great Northern (Samaritan) sanctuaries.'[109] No evidence links the Samaritans with Bethel, and this is simply a case of the use of the term 'Samaritan' to denote any opposition to the Jerusalem Jews during this period of restoration. Foster is much more likely to be on the right lines when he notes that 'the attempt to discredit the embassage from Bethel is clear'.[110]

Only one other passage in Zechariah 1–8 calls for consideration

[106] Murphy, art. cit., p. 686. (My italics.)
[107] Ackroyd, *Exile and Restoration*, pp. 206ff.
[108] IB, VI, p. 1083.
[109] Foster, op. cit., p. 109.
[110] Ibid., p. 109, note 2.

here. The third of the visions, in 2:1-5 (MT. 2:5-9), with its description of the measuring of Jerusalem and its assurance of Yahweh's protection of the city, has sometimes been understood in a 'political' sense. The suggestion has been made that the background to this vision was a Samaritan threat against Jerusalem, which the leaders of the community wished to forestall by rebuilding the city walls, whereas Zechariah's vision warns against this reliance on human defences. This would be a false material trust which would strengthen the Samaritan case with the imperial authorities.[111] Such a suggestion obviously cannot be disproved, but there are a number of major objections to it. If a 'political' interpretation be allowed for the vision, we must once again remember that we have no supporting knowledge of any kind as to what particular circumstances may have underlain it. Even if some attack similar to that of which we read in Nehemiah's time was involved, it would be the imperial authorities in Samaria, anxious to retain the fullness of their power against any rival claim being made for Jerusalem, who would most probably have been involved. In fact, however, it may be doubted whether any 'political' interpretation is called for at all. It is more natural to suppose that this is a general description of God's promise to his city, 'a message of the nature of the new city, which will spread abroad in the land, protected by the presence of God himself'.[112]

Before leaving this period of restoration, we may consider briefly another recent discussion which has argued that Samaritan influence may be traced at this period. I. H. Eybers contributed an article to a collection of South African *Biblical Essays* in which he argued that the division between Samaritans and Jews took place in this period, and was occasioned by the return of some of the exiled Jews following the decree of Cyrus.[113] Eybers follows the 'Samaritan' interpretation of those passages which have already been

[111] Slightly varying interpretations along these lines are proposed by Browne, op. cit., pp. 64f., and by Winton Thomas, IB, VI, p. 1064.

[112] Ackroyd, *Exile and Restoration*, p. 179. The suggestion that a Samaritan reference might be seen in the 'mountain' of Zech. 4.7 (so Elliger, ATD, p. 118), is listed by Ackroyd (op. cit., p. 173, note 8), among other 'extravagances of interpretation'.

[113] I. H. Eybers, 'Relations between Jews and Samaritans in the Persian Period', in *Biblical Essays: Proceedings of the Ninth Meeting of the Ou-Testamentiese Werkgemeenskap in Suid-Afrika*, 1966, p. 73.

discussed in Haggai and Zechariah, but differs from others who have taken that view, in that he sees a religious rather than a political motivation in the division.

Without setting out his arguments in detail, three comments may be made on Eybers' thesis. First, in order to establish his point that there was a sharp religious difference between those who returned from exile and those whom they encountered in Palestine, Eybers uses the common, but very dubious, procedure of supplying the gaps in Haggai and Zechariah by using the material from Ezra 4:1–5. This difficult section reflects the Chronicler's viewpoint, and while it may well contain historical information, it should not be taken as a straightforward account of the late sixth century.

Secondly, Eybers fails to give sufficient attention to the character of Samaritanism. At times, indeed, it appears as if any group opposed to the Jerusalem community may be labelled Samaritan. Thus in Ezra 4:1 there is reference to 'the adversaries of Judah and Benjamin', whom Eybers regards, reasonably enough, as the population living around Jerusalem, but whom he then goes on, quite gratuitously, to identify with the Samaritans.[114] Neither the religious character of Samaritanism, nor the geographical area in which they were found, can support such an identification.

Thirdly, it is noteworthy that Eybers' view, like others noticed in this section, is not based on either Jewish or Samaritan tradition concerning the date of a supposed schism. Nevertheless, such theories postulate a sudden and dramatic event, but one which is unsupported by any clear cut contemporary evidence, since only the most obscure allusions to it can be found, and which is wholly unsupported by later traditions concerning the nature and date of the cleavage. If both Jewish and Samaritan testimony concerning the origin of their division must be rejected as unreliable—and here one may agree with Eybers that it must be—then historically quite a different kind of presentation of the development becomes more plausible, with a gradual drifting apart rather than a sharp break.

We may conclude, therefore, that no genuine references to the Samaritans can be found in these sixth-century passages. Those interpretations which do so have in common that they approach

[114] Ibid., p. 73.

Samaritanism simply from the later Jewish point of view, rather than through what we know of its own distinctive features. Just as in the Fourth Gospel, 'the Jews' could accuse Jesus, 'You are a Samaritan and have a demon' (John 8:47), as if the two charges were complementary, so modern scholars have sometimes regarded any opposition to the Jerusalem Jews or any allegation of syncretistic practice as applicable to the Samaritans *tout court*, without further elucidation of the historical or religious situation.

## Nehemiah

The discussion thus far will have shown that there are still a number of scholars who regard it as legitimate to speak of 'Samaritans' as a clearly defined and identifiable group set over against the 'Jews' in this early post-exilic period which we have been considering. Even where this view is held, however, it is usually agreed that no decisive break had taken place by this period. If, as has been argued here, it is not yet appropriate to speak of Samaritanism in the sixth century, then clearly we must pass on to the next period of which the Old Testament gives evidence. It is usually agreed that that period is the middle of the fifth century.

It is not our concern here to enter into that much-debated question, the chronological order of Ezra and Nehemiah. The material available is not arranged in such a way as to provide a confident answer, and the debate will no doubt continue. The priority of Nehemiah seems the more likely, and is now very widely accepted as probable, and it will be accepted here, though no major issue turns on it in our present study. Of the many treatments of this question, the detailed examination by H. H. Rowley[115] remains probably the fullest, though there are certain dimensions of the problem, such as the nature of history in the work of the Chronicler, which are not entirely satisfactorily dealt with by Rowley's article.

The date of Nehemiah's first mission to Jerusalem is now generally agreed to have been 445 B.C. On other aspects of our

[115] Rowley, 'The Chronological Order of Ezra and Nehemiah', in *The Servant of the Lord* (Oxford, 2nd ed., 1965), pp. 137–68.

knowledge there is less agreement; for example, whether his was a unique role, or whether he was one in a series of governors;[116] whether what is sometimes called the 'Nehemiah memoir' is properly so described, or whether Nehemiah 1–6 is better described as a memorial in his honour.[117] In any case, however, it seems clear that he had important dealings with the imperial authorities in Samaria, and notably with Sanballat. This confrontation is very frequently pictured in Judaeo-Samaritan terms, but to speak of Sanballat as a Samaritan is to ignore a number of the distinctions which we have attempted to make in this study.

The Samaritans are most readily defined as a religious group centred upon Shechem. Sanballat is in quite a different situation. To appreciate his significance, we need once again to remember the distinction already noted between the representatives of the imperial government and the native population of the old northern kingdom. The administrative structure set up by the Assyrians nearly three centuries earlier was apparently largely maintained in its broad outlines, and Samaria continued to be the capital of an imperial province. It is not explicitly stated in the biblical record that Sanballat was the governor at Samaria, but it seems to be implicit in the account of Nehemiah's dealings with him, and is even more clearly implied in the Elephantine papyri, one of which refers to a letter sent 'to Delaiah and Shelemiah, the sons of Sanballat the governor of Samaria'.[118] The exact status of those mentioned in Nehemiah as allies of Sanballat—Tobiah and Geshem—is less clear, partly because there is here no external supporting evidence, but it is at least likely that they were governors respectively of Ammon and of some form of Arab confederacy.[119] Their opposition to Nehemiah appears to have been based on political grounds, and in particular the fear that their own status and power would be diminished if new privileges were to be awarded to Jerusalem. In studying the Old Testament it is often

---

[116] Cf. above, pp. 52f.

[117] Ackroyd, *Israel under Babylon and Persia*, pp. 247f.

[118] 'Petition to Bagoas', line 29; translated in *Documents from Old Testament Times*, p. 264.

[119] The suggestion of G. M. Landes (*IDB*, I, p. 113, under 'Ammon'), that there was originally reference made here to 'Abd the Ammonite, has not been widely followed, though the description of Tobiah as an Ammonite raises problems. Is it to be understood as a slighting reference?

dangerous to attempt to differentiate too precisely between political and religious affairs, but the account of the opposition to Nehemiah seems not to bring out any religious difference in the narrower sense, despite the plea to the contrary by Eybers.[120]

The difference between the Samaritans and the opponents of Nehemiah can now be spelt out more fully. Sanballat is seen as linked with other political leaders; Samaritanism would eschew such links. Sanballat is associated with the high-priestly line in Jerusalem (Neh. 13:28), and by inference with its Temple; such associations would have been utterly alien to the Samaritans, even though attempts have been made to see a Samaritan link in this episode. (It will be considered below, when we come to consider the evidence of Josephus.) Nothing is known of the religious aspect of Sanballat's policy, though the Elephantine papyrus just quoted shows that his sons were given Yahwistic names, so that it is apparently no more than conjecture when Bright suggests that his religion was 'surely somewhat syncretistic'.[121] Part of the difficulty here lies in the fact that it is apparently no longer possible at this period to deduce religious practice from the names that were given, and it is noteworthy that while Sanballat's sons had Yahwistic names, his own in the form in which it has come down to us is presumably a corruption of the Babylonian name Sinuballit (Sin has given life).

Two other points may be briefly noted in connection with Nehemiah, both of a somewhat negative kind. The first is that no mention is made in the Nehemiah material of Shechem or of Mount Gerizim, nor is there any implication that Nehemiah's opponents had Shechemite links of any kind, in any tradition earlier than the Josephus story already mentioned. The second point is the complete absence of any reference to Nehemiah in the Samaritan traditions, apart from some allusions in the Chronicle II which appear to be based upon the biblical material. In part this silence may be connected with the tendency, which will be noted

[120] Art. cit., p. 77. A valuable survey of Nehemiah's achievement and its implications is found in B. Reicke, *The New Testament Era* (London, 1969), pp. 19–23.

[121] Bright, op. cit., p. 383, following a suggestion by Albright. Rowley, 'Sanballat and the Samaritan Temple', in *Men of God*, p. 247, note 2, is rightly more cautious. In fact we know nothing of Sanballat's religious practice.

Esj

again, for the Nehemiah and Ezra traditions to exist parallel to one another, but with little overlapping; but at least we should be warned against the supposition that any decisive shift in Judaeo-Samaritan relations was due to the policy of Nehemiah.

## Ezra and the Chronicler

If the Samaritans' own tradition is silent with regard to Nehemiah, the situation concerning Ezra is very different. His influence came to be regarded as decisive by both Samaritans and Jews in the shaping of the later situation. This importance can most conveniently be illustrated by considering the significance of the Ezra-tradition at three levels: first, the mission of the man himself; secondly, the viewpoint of the book of Ezra and more generally of the Chronicler; and finally the place of Ezra in later tradition, both Jewish and Samaritan.

The precise nature and purpose of Ezra's mission have long been matters of dispute, to the extent that some scholars have cast doubts upon his very existence.[122] Such an attitude seems to be too negative, but we may properly recognize that a number of aspects of his mission remain unclear. The date at which it took place is still disputed, as has been noted already in considering the chronological relation between Ezra and Nehemiah. Probably the most satisfactory answer is to retain the reference in Ezra 7:7f. to 'the seventh year of Artaxerxes the king', and to understand the king in question as Artaxerxes II (404–358), and to place Ezra's mission in 398 B.C.

Of more relevance for our present purpose is the nature of Ezra's mission. It is not clear whether it should be seen as the 'religious' counterpart of the more 'political' concerns of Nehemiah, or whether the two men should be understood as carrying out essentially similar tasks with regard to the political status of Judah. Certainly the early years of Artaxerxes II were a time of unrest in the south-western part of the Persian Empire, as is illustrated by the loss of Egypt in 401, and the Elephantine papyri provide vivid illustration of the uncertainty of the period, especially for

[122] See the discussion in R. H. Pfeiffer, *Introduction to the Old Testament* (London, 1952), pp. 824–8.

those associated in Egyptian eyes with foreign rule. Of the situation in Palestine the Old Testament is our only source of knowledge, so it must remain a matter of speculation whether one of Ezra's tasks was to ensure the peace and stability of the region. We may have one pointer in that direction in the description of his position in the Aramaic document at Ezra 7:12: 'the scribe of the law of the God of heaven'. This is now commonly held to conceal a Persian imperial title, 'secretary, adviser for questions of the Jewish religion'—a description which may, in the manner of such titles, give a slightly more elevated impression of its bearer's status than was originally the case.[123] One could readily suppose, if Ezra had a court function of this kind, that his primary task was to ensure that there were no disturbances in Judah, and he would rightly be seen as a successor of Nehemiah in the sense that both men had essentially similar roles to perform.

An attempt has recently been made to spell out the implications of Ezra's mission in terms analogous to this. J. G. Vink, in his study of the Priestly Code,[124] has gone against the recent tendency to date the Priestly Code in about the sixth century, and has argued that it should be seen as the pivotal point of Ezra's mission. He accepts the 398 dating for Ezra, and supposes that the Persian authorities, anxious to maintain peace on their south-western borders, were concerned to conciliate Jews and Samaritans. On this view the role of Ezra was not, as has commonly been held, anti-Samaritan, but rather was designed to remove possible hostility by allowing some of their claims against the Jews of Jerusalem. Thus Joshua 8:30–35, the description of the building of an altar on Mount Ebal by Joshua, is ascribed to P and seen as a deliberate modification of the existing Deuteronomic law which was regarded as allowing only one altar, that in Jerusalem.

The main concern in Vink's study is with the Priestly Code, and this is not directly relevant to the present inquiry. Both literary and methodological objections have been raised against it: the ascription of Joshua 8:30ff. and other sections of that book to P is now widely doubted; and the method of treating the historical situation is often that of *ignotum per ignotius*. It is simply not

---

[123] See Eissfeldt, op. cit., p. 556, and Ackroyd, *Israel under Babylon and Persia*, pp. 267f.
[124] J. G. Vink, *The Date and Origin of the Priestly Code* (Leiden, 1969).

possible to reconstruct with such confidence the historical situation
underlying Ezra's mission. Two objections to Vink's approach
in so far as it concerns the Samaritans may briefly be noted: the
first is the difficulty of explaining the hatred with which Ezra
came later to be regarded by the Samaritans if the purpose of his
mission was in fact conciliatory towards them; the second is that
Vink fails to make any distinction between 'Samarians' and
Samaritans. He follows Alt in recognizing the importance of the
'socio-political superstructure'[125] in Samaria, but fails to make the
necessary distinction between this group and the later Samaritans,
whose religious practice, political affiliation and geographical
location were all different.

Vink's account of events, therefore—though it has many
interesting points of detail—must be regarded as unsatisfactory
in its attempt to relate Ezra, the Priestly Code and the Samaritans
within one complex of events. Indeed, it is noteworthy that the
biblical account of Ezra's mission, although the presentation is in
markedly 'religious' terms, gives no indication of why the reforms
he carried out should have had any significance *vis-à-vis* Samaritanism. Yet it remains the fact that Ezra is regarded by both
Jewish and Samaritan tradition as a figure of great importance.
This seeming inconsistency is taken up by Rowley in his study
of Samaritan origins, and it is to his reconstruction that we now
turn.[126]

He starts from the point just noted, that 'it is curious that the
Samaritans are nowhere mentioned in the Bible in connection
with Ezra, and yet in Samaritan tradition Ezra is associated with
the schism more bitterly than is Nehemiah'. Rowley regards
Ezra's mission as primarily concerned with religious purity, and
in particular with ensuring the community's acceptance of the
law that he brought with him, which may well have been either
the Priestly Code or the complete Pentateuch. On this reconstruction, a further compromise on the matter of true priesthood was
involved, which was unacceptable to the Samaritans. Thus
Rowley's conclusion is that, mainly as a result of this disagreement
on the priesthood, 'the division between the Jews and the Samari-

[125] Vink's expression (op. cit., p. 18).
[126] *The Samaritan Schism in Legend and History*. The quotations are
from pp. 218f.

tans, which had developed in the reign of Artaxerxes I and had taken on a religious flavour because of the growing segregation between the two communities, appears to have sharpened and to have become linked more definitely with religion, though it was in no sense fundamentally religious in its origin. The two communities continued to drift ever more and more apart.'

This proposed reconstruction both brings out valuable insights and also raises difficulties. It is important for the recognition that the nature and proper exercise of true priesthood was one of the basic causes of difference between Jews and Samaritans, and this is a point to which we shall have to make reference again. Also important is Rowley's characterization of the division as a 'drifting apart'; this, rather than a sudden and dramatic schism, certainly seems best to explain the separation that developed. Other aspects of his reconstruction are, however, more problematic. The reference to developments in the reign of Artaxerxes I (that is, during the mission of Nehemiah) involves that ambiguity in the use of the term 'Samaritan' which we have already had cause to notice, and Rowley uses the term in describing Sanballat and his supporters, whereas, as we saw at the outset, 'Samarians' would be more appropriate.[127] There are further assumptions made concerning the role and achievement of Ezra himself which are strictly no more than hypotheses. Thus, the statement that Ezra made a compromise on the priesthood which proved unacceptable to the Samaritans has no direct support either in the Old Testament or in Samaritan tradition. It depends on three further unstated assumptions: first, that the 'book of the law' referred to (Neh. 8:1, etc.) was either the Priestly Code or the complete Pentateuch; secondly, that Ezra was in a position to put its requirements into practice right away; and thirdly, that he met opposition to his measures from a group who can be identified with the Samaritans. All three of these assumptions involve major difficulties. In the first place the identification of 'the book of the law' remains far from clear—nor indeed is it apparent that the attempt to identify it either with the whole Pentateuch or with some definable stratum thereof is a legitimate procedure.[128] Secondly, the description of

[127] Above, p. 9.
[128] Cf. the methodological warnings of Ackroyd, *Israel under Babylon and Persia*, pp. 273f.

the reforms which followed the reading of the law make no mention of anything in the realm of priesthood, but are concerned rather with the correct observance of the festivals. Thirdly, while some opposition to the work of Ezra is indeed recorded, it is in connection with his enactment concerning mixed marriages (Ezra 10:15) rather than with the reading of the law-book. Nor is there anything to associate it with Samaritans or with anyone outside the Jerusalem community. It would appear that the situation here was similar to that which we observed in the time of Haggai, with division and resultant condemnation within the Jerusalem community itself. There is therefore no evidence in what can be traced of the mission of Ezra to point to any significant Judaeo-Samaritan development associated with his work.

The mission of Ezra himself, however, is only dealt with in the last four chapters of the book of Ezra. To look at the viewpoint of the whole book will help to lead into our second main consideration in examining the Ezra-tradition—the viewpoint of the Chronicler. Some scholars, notably W. F. Albright,[129] have argued that Ezra was himself the Chronicler, while others reject the view that the books of Ezra and Nehemiah have a common origin with 1 and 2 Chronicles.[130] The view here taken is the common one that these books are the product of one closely-knit group, which we may by a convenient shorthand already used several times in this study call 'the Chronicler'. It was probably in this milieu that Haggai and Zechariah 1–8 were put into something like their present form. Before the attempt is made to assess the purpose of the Chronicler in more general terms, to see whether any light is thrown on Samaritanism, some consideration may properly be given to the presentation in Ezra 1–6 of the events of the period from the time of Cyrus to the building of the Second Temple.

These events have already been under consideration in connection with the study of Haggai and Zechariah 1–8, but certain significant differences emerge in the way that they are presented in these chapters, so that a further study is necessary. Not only is

---

[129] In a number of works: most recently, *Yahweh and the Gods of Canaan* (London, 1968), p. 158.

[130] So S. Japhet, 'The Supposed Common Authorship of Chronicles and Ezra-Nehemiah investigated anew', *VT*, XVIII, 3, 1968, pp. 330–71.

too ready a cross-reference from Haggai and Zechariah to Ezra 1–6 methodologically dangerous, but there is also a further reason why it is desirable to consider Ezra 1–6 in the same section as 7–10. In the book of Ezra the restoration of the true Israel to its true home in Jerusalem is presented as a unity; the passage of what may be a considerable span of time is reduced to 'now after this' (Ezra 7:1). and it even appears as if Ezra is himself presented as belonging to the next generation after that which was taken into exile, when he is named as 'son of Seraiah' (7:1; cf. 2 Kings 25:18). This overriding unity of theme and apparent disregard of historical precision will be very important in our study of Ezra 4 in particular. It is only by the recognition of a basic underlying theological purpose, to illustrate the nature of the opposition which the community encountered and the providence of their God in guiding them safely through it, that sense can be made of this chapter with its switch from Hebrew to Aramaic, its literary-critical problems, and its historical perplexities. These difficulties, of course, remain; but they are seen in their proper proportion if the over-riding theme is given due recognition, and it is in this chapter that possible Samaritan allusions have been found.

The basic question here, of course, is the identity of the opposition here described: was it from a distinct group whose identity can be recovered? or have different occasions of tension been drawn together as illustrative of the one over-riding theological principle? The variety of names used to describe those who opposed the work of restoration, and the different situations implied by the rather allusive historical references, suggests that the latter possibility is more likely, and that the Chronicler has brought together several originally distinct traditions under the general head of 'opposition to the true community'. If this is so, it will be extremely hazardous to attempt to decide either the original historical situation or the exact composition of the various opposition groups, though some suggestions may be possible. Thus, in vv. 1–3 two obvious possibilities suggest themselves: if a genuine historical reminiscence is preserved here, then it will be appropriate to link this with the events of Esarhaddon's reign already referred to in the consideration of Isaiah 7:8.[131] In this case the opposition could be traced to the 'Samarians', that is,

[131] Above, p. 23.

those established in Samaria as an official governing class, and the situation underlying this passage would be one in which the bureaucracy in Samaria was anxious to keep an eye on developments in Jerusalem. (An additional problem here is that in the corresponding passage in 1 Esdras (5:69), the Greek form of the name of the Assyrian king is Asbasareth. It is not clear whether this represents an independent tradition; Torrey has suggested a process by which this might be a corruption of an original form Esarhaddon.[132])

Many scholars, on the other hand, have supposed that this is not a genuine historical reminiscence at all, but simply an invention of the Chronicler. If this is so, we may note simply that this provides further evidence that the picture in 2 Kings 17 of a once-for-all settlement in the eighth century is not shared by other parts of the Old Testament; and that if this section is intended to be anti-Samaritan, it is remarkably allusive. Nothing in these verses shows in any clear way who were the adversaries being condemned, and this might provide a pointer to the Chronicler's purpose in more general terms. It is possible to understand his work as being aimed to uphold the claims of the Jerusalem community and to show how God worked with it, rather than to decry any specific rival. This seems more probable than the—surely over-subtle—suggestion of Torrey that the discrepancy between this passage and the account in 2 Kings 17 is an illustration of the Chronicler's shrewdness in making the Samaritans produce 'documentary evidence of their own "heathen" origin [which] would weigh all the heavier against them if it was manifestly independent of the Jewish tradition'.[133]

The following verses (Ezra 4:4f.) could be taken as referring to the same set of events, though in that case the changed description of those involved—formerly 'the adversaries of Judah and Benjamin', now 'the people of the land'—would be curious; or it may illustrate a different occasion of hostility. There have been various suggestions as to the identification of 'the people of the land' in this section,[134] but whatever view is adopted, there is

[132] Torrey, *Ezra Studies* (New York, 1970 (= 10)), p. 169, note 41.
[133] Ibid., p. 169.
[134] See Coggins, 'The Interpretation of Ezra IV 4', *JTS*, NS, XVI, 1965, pp. 124–7, and Ackroyd, *Exile and Restoration*, p. 150, note 50.

no reason to link them with the Samaritans. As in Haggai, the opposition appears to consist of local rather than northern groups. In this respect I should still wish to maintain what I wrote some years ago,[135] that the original reference was not to the Samaritans, but I should now wish to modify my then almost unquestioning assumption that the present intention of the passage was to identify the opposition with the Samaritans. As we shall see when we come to consider the purpose of the Chronicler more fully, such an identification may here, as with 4:1–3, be too precise, and may stress too greatly the negative aspects of his presentation.

The Aramaic section of this chapter raises yet more problems. The particular difficulty is vv. 9f., where the complainants to Artaxerxes are listed, first by titles, and then as 'the Persians, the men of Erech, the Babylonians, the men of Susa, that is, the Elamites, and the rest of the nations whom the great and mighty Osnappar deported and settled in the cities of Samaria and in the rest of the province Beyond the River'. Here, more clearly than elsewhere, it is the imperial officials who are involved, as is shown by the list of titles, and also by the variety of places implied throughout the empire. As to 'Osnappar', the majority of commentators take this as a corruption of Assur-banapal, and therefore a further indication of a variety of traditions underlying the importation of different groups into Samaria; the reading in Josephus 'Salmanasses' (*Ant.*, XI, 19), that is, the Assyrian king usually rendered as Shalmaneser in English, has been regarded as original by Torrey.[136] In this connection it is worth noting that here as elsewhere Josephus makes the identification of the community's enemies with the Samaritans a much more explicit one, by introducing his version of the episode with 'the surrounding nations, especially the Chuthaeans'.[137]

In summary, it appears that any historical occasions of conflict which may underlie the present form of this chapter are not likely to have had any connection with the Samaritans. In Josephus, such a connection is clearly stated. Where does the Chronicler stand? The commonly-held view that he too was concerned to

---

[135] See previous note.

[136] *Ezra Studies*, pp. 169f.

[137] *Antiquities* XI, 19. 'Chuthaeans' is, as has already been noted (p. 10, above), one of Josephus' regular descriptions of the Samaritans.

attack the Samaritans cannot be excluded by the form of this chapter, but equally it is certainly not the only conclusion to which we are led. The question can only be decided by trying to obtain an overall impression of his purpose.

Viewed positively, it appears as if the Chronicler was looking back on the achievement of Ezra from the standpoint of a period perhaps a generation or so later, and regarded it as the fulfilment of all God's promises to Jerusalem. That promise was associated especially with the choice of David (1 Chron. 10–29), but could ultimately be traced back as far as Abraham, through the identification of the site of the Temple with that of Abraham's projected sacrifice of Isaac (2 Chron. 3:1). There is, therefore, a very positive evaluation of Jerusalem as the chosen place of Yahweh. Some illustrations of this in the post-exilic period have already been noted here; it pervades the whole of the Chronicler's work. In this respect, it is in line with the view of the Deuteronomists as expressed in Samuel and Kings, though there are also undoubted differences of emphasis. In the Deuteronomic work, as we have seen,[138] there is a consistently hostile attitude to the Northern kingdom, and this is again found in the Chronicler, for whom it was a rival to Jerusalem in both political and religious terms. The Chronicler, however, expresses his hostility in a somewhat different way from the Deuteronomist. Whereas the books of Kings lose no opportunity of stressing the wickedness of the Northern rulers and the fact that the very existence of that kingdom was an affront to true Yahwism, the Chronicler's method of underlining the fact that the true worship of Yahweh could be practised—and had always been practised—only at Jerusalem was to omit almost all the references to the Northern Kingdom which he found in his sources. Even in those examples of opposition to the people of Judah which we have noted in the book of Ezra, we have observed that it is only in a very indirect way that they are associated with the survivors of the old Northern kingdom.

That this eagerness to maintain the claims of Jerusalem was complemented by—and indeed probably occasioned by—rival claims on behalf of other interpretations of true Yahwism is scarcely to be doubted. Part of the Chronicler's intention was therefore polemical, as commentators have regularly recognized.

[138] Above, p. 28.

But the identification of those against whom this polemic was directed is a good deal less clear. Most commonly it has been held that it was the Samaritans who were the objects of his condemnation. Such a view could be held without difficulty in precritical days, when the story in 2 Kings 17 was accepted at its face value, and in more recent times it was set out in a modified form by Torrey, whose views on this point have received more support than many of his other interpretations of Old Testament themes. The basis of Torrey's interpretation of the Chronicler was twofold; the positive side, which we have already considered, 'to establish beyond all question the supremacy of the mother church . . . was the impulse, primarily, which produced the whole "history" which the Chronicler wrote';[139] and the negative side, to reject the Samaritan claim that they were the true Israel.

With the positive evaluation we have already expressed agreement; the negative side is less convincing. Torrey himself admitted that the polemic was 'half-concealed', and suggested that the Chronicler 'was of course much too shrewd a man to introduce into his history any open polemic against the Samaritans'.[140] Such an admission considerably reduces the force of the original point. It is also important to bear in mind that Torrey took the likely date of the Chronicler as *c.* 250, at a time when the Samaritan Temple on Mount Gerizim had been built, and its rival claims were openly being asserted; on the usual view, that the Chronicler was active *c.* 350, this point also loses much of its force.

Despite these limitations, however, Torrey's basic point of view has been followed. Thus Rowley, who is elsewhere critical of Torrey, reaches the same conclusion on this point: '[the Chronicler] betrays an anti-Samaritan bias which cannot be mistaken'.[141] Many other scholars have expressed basically similar views. Nevertheless, such conclusions must to a large extent be argued from silence, simply because of the paucity of Northern references in the Chronicler's work. It is also important to bear in mind that our increasing knowledge of Judaism in the last centuries B.C. suggests that a simple 'Jews *v.* Samaritans' presentation may be something of an over-simplification. It may be better to say that the beginnings of Samaritanism represented one only of the

---

[139] *Ezra Studies*, p. 153.     [140] Ibid., p. 235.
[141] Rowley, *The Samaritan Schism in Legend and History*, p. 219.

rivalries which the Chronicler saw as a dangerous alternative to that worship of Yahweh which for his school could only be carried out properly at Jerusalem. I have already elsewhere suggested an approach to the Chronicler along these lines,[142] and the point is carried a stage further by Ackroyd. He says: 'It is certainly right to consider how far later, more rigid descriptions are really appropriate to the period in which [the Chronicler] was active. The aims of the Chronicler may certainly be described as polemical, but it may be better to describe them as being in favour of a certain type of interpretation of the ancestral faith rather than as being representative of "orthodoxy" contrasted with "schism" or "heresy".'[143]

We may attempt to summarize the Chronicler's purpose in this respect, therefore, by starting from the fact that he regarded the pre-eminence of Jerusalem as an essential requirement for the unity of Judaism. Because of this, he is therefore opposed to all those fissiparous tendencies which might, in his view, endanger that unity. The predominance of cultic material and interest in the work of the Chronicler make it natural to suppose that the particular way in which he saw these fissiparous tendencies as a threat was in the sphere of the cult. It may not have been necessary at the time of the Chronicler to argue for the legitimacy of worship at the Jerusalem sanctuary—though, as will be seen, both the Samaritan evidence and the viewpoint of some of the Qumran material suggest the possibility of a different conclusion—but he wished to go beyond that, and stress not only the legitimacy of the Jerusalem sanctuary, but also its uniqueness as the only place proper for the worship of Yahweh. Such an assertion needed to be established by being presented as an integral part of Israel's past history. In such a situation one—but only one—of the divisive elements about which the Chronicler was concerned would be those who upheld the claims of Mount Gerizim. It would be anachronistic to picture the fourth century situation in terms of Jews and Samaritans as two clearly-defined, opposed groups, whose rivalries sufficiently account for all the tensions and cross-currents within Judaism.

[142] Coggins, 'The Old Testament and Samaritan Origins', *ASTI*, VI, pp. 35–48, esp. pp. 45f.
[143] Ackroyd, *Exile and Restoration*, p. 236, note 12.

In the light of such a presentation it becomes possible to look again at some of those passages considered earlier, where the possibility of a 'Samaritan' interpretation was left open, to see how they agree with this understanding. With regard to Abijah's speech in 2 Chronicles 13,[144] this can be seen as fitting into the outline just suggested; the claims of the Jerusalem sanctuary are strongly upheld against all forms of division, and the argument on behalf of the Jerusalem cult would be valid against any rival claims. That such claims were made on behalf of northern sanctuaries seems to be implicit here, and one such—though not necessarily the only one—could well have been Mount Gerizim. A very similar interpretation would apply to the story in 2 Chronicles 30, though the differentiation there between the Ephraimites who 'laughed them to scorn' and those in Asher, Manasseh and Zebulun who 'humbled themselves and came to Jerusalem' (vv. 10f.) may point to a more conciliatory attitude towards some whom it was hoped to bring within the Jerusalem fold and greater hostility towards those in Ephraim, so that here a more specifically anti-Samaritan attitude might be traceable. But, as has already been noted,[145] the reconstruction here is complicated by our lack of knowledge of the original historical circumstances. In addition, it will be recalled, the attempt to work out a more precise link with the Samaritans was dependent upon an unusually late date for the Chronicler.[146] Another point which was left open at an earlier stage until further consideration had been given to the Chronicler's purpose was the editorial framework of Haggai (and Zech. 1–8), on the assumption that that framework can be traced to a Chronistic milieu.[147] In these passages the emphasis seems to be rather on the positive importance of Jerusalem than on any particular rival claims, and in these books neither the original prophetic words nor the setting in which they have now been placed can justifiably be called anti-Samaritan.

One last point must be made with regard to the tendency to see anything more than the very beginnings of anti-Samaritan polemic, and that within a larger context, in the work of the Chronicler. This portrayal, where it involves a breach between Jews and

---

[144] Cf. above, pp. 11f.    [145] Above, pp. 20f.
[146] Cf. the summary of, and comments on, Kraus' view on p. 21, above.
[147] Cf. pp. 49, 52, above.

Samaritans in the time of Ezra or earlier, seems to involve an extremely complex historical process, for it brings together data which are basically incompatible. It is necessary, on such a view, to suppose on the one hand that there had been a decisive breach between Jews and Samaritans, yet on the other to recognize that Samaritanism was influenced by, and shared many of the characteristics of, Judaism down to the second or first centuries B.C., or even into the Christian era, as was seen at the outset. Such a view is found, somewhat surprisingly, in the work of Purvis. He recognizes the gradual nature of the developing breach between Jews and Samaritans, and yet still considers that the real basic occasion of a Samaritan schism can be traced as early as the sixth century B.C.[148] When due consideration is given to the common Jewish and Samaritan devotion to the Pentateuch, and the number of beliefs held in common which are characteristic of the later period of Judaism, it is scarcely likely that these will have been separate developments by independent groups. They were rather the product of a common inheritance within Judaism.

It is time to return to Ezra. Some attention has now been paid to two aspects of his importance for our study: his actual historical situation, and the presentation of his work by the Chronicler. A third aspect remains for consideration—the place of Ezra in subsequent tradition. Many figures in the ancient world are as important for the tradition which developed around them after their lifetime as for what can be reconstructed of their actual achievement. The Old Testament offers many examples of this situation; and Ezra is one such. By the Jews he came to be accorded a place of honour second only to that of Moses, whereas in Samaritan tradition he was regarded with deep hostility.

The particular importance of Ezra within Judaism came to be associated especially with the development of the idea of a canon of scripture, though there is little enough solid evidence for this tradition in the historical sources available to us. The grounds for Samaritan hostility are not much clearer. To some extent it is based on his exclusivist policy, but the real gravamen of their complaint appears to be that Ezra had tampered with the traditional script, and—more serious still—had falsified the text itself.[149]

[148] Op. cit., pp. 98f.
[149] Gaster, *The Samaritans*, pp. 26–29.

Ezra, that is, is regarded as being responsible for the introduction of the square Aramaic script for Hebrew, as well as emending certain key Pentateuchal texts, especially Deuteronomy 27:4, by substituting 'Ebal' for 'Gerizim', and so derogating from the sanctity of the Samaritans' holy place. Many modern scholars regard the Samaritan claim to have preserved the original reading here as a justifiable one,[150] but the historicity of the allegation that these changes should be associated with Ezra must remain doubtful. It is impossible by normal historical methods to trace back any significant role in the formation of a canon to Ezra. The Pentateuch can scarcely have reached its present form long before Ezra's time, and it is as sacred to the Samaritan as to the Jew.

Ezra's real significance, it is clear, is symbolic. No specific charges brought against him can be upheld, but he, more than anyone else, stands for the exclusiveness of Judaism. Still more important and more specific, Ezra represents an exclusiveness based on Jerusalem and its claims to a unique status. It was this traditional picture of Ezra which made him so unacceptable a figure to the later Samaritans, and caused him to be so greatly venerated by later Jews.

Thus far the assumption has been made that this veneration was as universal among the Jews as was his denigration among the Samaritans. In fact, this appears not to have been the case, and we are reminded once more of the complexity of Judaism, and the danger of setting up a Jerusalemite 'orthodoxy' looking back to Ezra as the norm by comparison with which all else could be judged schismatic or heretical. U. Kellermann has shown in a detailed study of the Nehemiah tradition in the Old Testament and in post-biblical literature that in certain circles traditions grew up concerning the work and importance of Nehemiah, traditions which were no doubt rooted in historical facts but which often elaborated or distorted them in the course of time. Such traditions can be traced in such passages as Ecclesiasticus 49:13, 2 Maccabees 1:18ff. and probably 1 Enoch 89:72. The passage in 2 Maccabees

---

[150] Cf. the *apparatus criticus* to *Biblia Hebraica*, ed. R. Kittel, 3rd edn. Some further consideration is given to the significance of the Samaritan Pentateuch in establishing Samaritan origins in chapter 5 below, pp. 148–55.

is of particular interest because of the elaboration of Nehemiah's role in rebuilding the Temple and its altar, and in rekindling the sacred fire. In none of these passages does Ezra play any part at all, while in another apocryphal work, 1 Esdras, the portion referring to Nehemiah (5:40) is quite separate from that concerned with Ezra.[151] No conclusive argument can be based on these facts, but at least a good case can be made for the view that in some circles within Judaism it was not Ezra but Nehemiah (sometimes linked, as in Ecclesiasticus, with Zerubbabel) whose role was decisive. If the view first put forward by K. Galling and supported by Ackroyd and others be accepted, that the Nehemiah material was not incorporated into the complete corpus Chronicles-Ezra-Nehemiah until a late stage in its development, this would be additional evidence along the same lines.[152] In any case we are once again warned against too neat a 'Jews and Samaritans' division.

## The Hellenistic Period

It is not likely that there is any Old Testament evidence later than the work of the Chronicler that will be relevant to our present purpose. It is very probable that Daniel, and quite likely that some other Old Testament books, as a whole or in part, had yet to be composed, but none of those which are usually regarded as coming from this late period offers any evidence concerning Samaritanism—not even the account in Daniel 11, which is generally taken to be an outline of the history of Palestine from the time of Alexander the Great to that of Antiochus IV Epiphanes. Arguments from silence always need to be treated with caution; but at least this lack of reference warns us against supposing that overwhelming hostility against the Samaritans was a major influence in the development of Judaism at this period.

It has, however, been suggested from time to time that hidden references to this obscure period may be found in certain Old

---

[151] U. Kellermann, 'Nehemiah: Quellen, Überlieferung, und Geschichte', *BZAW*, 102; Berlin, 1967.

[152] Galling, *Chronik, Esra, Nehemia*, ATD, Göttingen, 1954; Ackroyd, *Exile and Restoration*, pp. 139, 236f.

Testament books, and that hostility to the Samaritans was an important factor in their composition. Torrey's late dating of the Chronicler may in a sense be taken as an instance of this; and it is appropriate at this point to give further consideration to Torrey's reconstruction of the history of this period, to which reference has already been made in connection with Ezekiel.[153] He argued that a considerable part of the Old Testament as it has come down to us reached its present form in the third century, and that Jewish-Samaritan hostility was one of the causes of its composition. For Torrey, the final editing of Jeremiah, Ezekiel and Second Isaiah all took place during the third century. Particularly significant here is his interpretation of the purpose of Ezekiel.

According to Torrey the book of Ezekiel in its original form was composed in the mid third century, as 'a pseudepigraph purporting to come from the reign of Manasseh'.[154] A little later, *c.* 230, it was transformed into the book as we have it, with its original setting now changed into one which claims the Babylonian exile as its background; and it was this transformation which was brought about as a piece of polemic against the Samaritans, as a result of their claim that the Jerusalemite traditions had been irredeemably broken by the destruction of the city in 586, and that the ritual practice of the contemporary Jerusalem cultus was of late and foreign origin. To counter this claim the theory of the Babylonian exile was developed, especially in the circle of the Chronicler, and so it came to be held that 'the genuine old tradition was preserved, entire and uncontaminated, by way of the deportation to Babylonia',[155] while Jerusalem itself remained unoccupied. In addition to the setting out of this theory in the work of the Chronicler, it was further elaborated by the false Babylonian setting given to Ezekiel, a setting which can, on Torrey's view, be identified as a series of easily detectable and removable glosses, some thirty in all being listed.[156] In this way the claims of Jerusalem were successfully maintained against those of the Samaritans at Gerizim.

---

[153] Above, p. 33.
[154] Torrey, *Pseudo-Ezekiel and the Original Prophecy* (1970 ( =30), New York), p. 102.
[155] Ibid., p. 103.
[156] Ibid., pp. 108–12.

Torrey's views are so idiosyncratic that it is unlikely that they would ever be followed in their entirety. That they have been influential is, nevertheless, undeniable. One or two other scholars have been markedly influenced by him in their interpretation of Ezekiel. Thus, for example, W. H. Brownlee has treated a single chapter of the book along comparable lines. In an examination of Ezekiel 13 he has argued that the original poetic material has been subjected to a prose redaction in the third century, whose purpose was to uphold the claims of the Jerusalem temple, its cultus and its priesthood as against the rival claims of the Samaritans.[157] It is an ingenious theory, and not easily disproved, but, among other difficulties, it is open to the same objection as other ingenious attempts to explain Old Testament passages in anti-Samaritan terms. As the passage stands it is extremely difficult to find anything that could be taken as anti-Samaritan: is propaganda of such subtlety of any value, and is it likely to have been used? The contrast with the straightforward condemnations of Josephus or even of Ecclesiasticus 50:26 is very marked.

It would seem that the result of Torrey's work has been to lead scholars to a great deal of fresh thought about the problems of the exile, and of the various reconstructions of Jewish history that are found in the Old Testament itself; but his solutions have won much less support. After an extended period when very drastic critical surgery because of the undoubted problems of the composition of Ezekiel was widely supported, the general tendency in more recent scholarship has been to suppose that the book contains a substantial nucleus of sixth-century material, and that there was a genuine prophet named Ezekiel active in Babylonia at that time. Nor have Torrey's views with regard to a supposed outburst of literary activity in the third century won support, and we must continue to admit ignorance of the history of that period. Finally, as far as the Samaritans are concerned, it is worth reiterating that Torrey's views did not attempt to explain the origin of the Samaritans, but took it for granted that in the crucial third century they were an established group, already in opposition to the Jews of Jerusalem. This opposition was based on rival claims concerning priesthood and on the existence of the sanctuary on Mount Geri-

[157] W. H. Brownlee, 'Exorcising the Souls from Ezekiel 13', *JBL*, 69, 1950, pp. 367–73.

zim as a rival to that of Jerusalem; and these are both subjects to which it will be necessary to return.[158]

The fact that one particular interpretation of the history of this later Old Testament period has generally been regarded with scepticism does not of course mean that we should, as it were, 'write off' the whole period as beyond our knowledge. It is certainly possible to discern a process of reinterpretation of older material, even if we are rarely able to be confident about that process in detail. In particular, it has often been suggested that particular passages from the older parts of the Old Testament have been given a fresh meaning, with particular reference to the Samaritans. In some cases this process is beyond dispute; 2 Kings 17 provides the classic example. But there are a number of other passages, where such a reinterpretation is much less clear, which are yet worth brief consideration as providing examples of the kind of material that may have been so understood.

One such passage is Psalm 78. Though certainty in dating Psalms is notoriously difficult to achieve, there is now a widespread view that this Psalm in its 'original' form—again the term may be question-begging!—was pre-exilic. However that may be, the references in the last verses to the choice of Judah, and specifically of Mount Zion and of David, and the rejection of the house of Joseph and the tribe of Ephraim (vv. 67ff.)—all of this could obviously be applied to the hostility between Jews and Samaritans at a later age. The point has been made by R. P. Carroll: '[the psalm's] function after the exile must have contributed greatly to the polemic directed against the Samaritan community. In that period the ancient traditions of the past had been reshaped to form the theologoumena of early Judaism.'[159] Whether it is right to go on to assert that the division between Jews and Samaritans was only a new form of the old controversy between Judah and Israel must be less certain, in view of the great Samaritan stress

---

[158] The reissue of Torrey's work includes the criticism that was made of it by S. Spiegel (originally published as 'Ezekiel or Pseudo-Ezekiel', in *HTR*, XXIV, 1931), and he recognized the Samaritan links in Ezekiel, though interpreting them in a fashion very different from that of Torrey. See esp. pp. 148–54.

[159] R. P. Carroll, 'Psalm LXXVIII: Vestiges of a Tribal Polemic', *VT* XXI, 2, 1971, p. 141.

on the difference between themselves and the 'eight tribes' whom
they describe as having constituted the Northern kingdom. But
the general sense of Psalm 78 certainly makes an interpretation
along these lines very probable. (An earlier verse in the same
Psalm, v. 9, might also, with its contemptuous reference to
Ephraim, be regarded as an anti-Samaritan gloss.)[160]

Another Psalm which very readily lends itself to the same kind
of interpretation is Psalm 87, especially v. 2, where the preferred
place of Zion in Yahweh's affection over 'all the dwelling-places of
Jacob' is asserted.[161] Either as the original purpose, if a late
date for this Psalm be assumed, or as a reinterpretation, if this is a
pre-exilic Psalm, anti-Samaritan polemic could well be recognized
here. At this point, however, a certain caution is necessary; very
many Psalms extol the praises of Zion, and this is often done by
means of a comparison with other, less favoured places. It would
be unwise to suppose that every such comparison concealed a
reference to the Samaritans, or even came to be interpreted in
such a way at a later period.

A passage of rather a different type where a Samaritan reinterpretation has been alleged is that concerning the shepherds in
Zechariah 11. This part of Zechariah is notoriously difficult to
date, and so it is not surprising that a variety of interpretations
has been suggested. We have already noted that Elliger finds a
number of Samaritan references in Haggai and Zechariah, and so
it is not surprising that he has taken this cryptic passage to refer
to the Samaritans.[162] This passage is then dated in the Greek
period, probably at the very end of the fourth century, and the
staffs are taken to refer to divisions within the covenant community,
and specifically to the schism brought about by the building of the
Samaritan Temple on Mount Gerizim. This interpretation is
followed also by Delcor, who sees in the name of the second staff
'ḥōḇelīm' (?bands ?union—the translation is disputed) an allusion

---

[160] This view was taken by A. Deissler, *Die Psalmen II*, Die Welt der
Bibel (Düsseldorf, 1964), p. 135, and is also found in the critical notes to
the Jerusalem Bible.

[161] Deissler, op. cit., p. 171.

[162] Elliger, op. cit., pp. 153f. This interpretation of the material has
been followed by a number of other scholars, and the Jerusalem Bible
critical notes, ad loc., suggest that this passage might be 'the earliest
evidence we have of the Samaritan schism'.

to Samaritanism.[163] The breaking of the staffs then becomes the symbol of a final schism. So difficult a passage is this that it has been interpreted in a great variety of ways. It may well be that the language here points to clear divisions within the community, but no more specific accusations are made here such as would fit in with what is known of Samaritanism. If a Samaritan view is appropriate here, it is more likely to be a matter of later reinterpretation than of the original purpose of the material.

These passages have been chosen as typical examples of the kind of material which lent itself to a fresh understanding in this way. It would obviously be impossible to work through the entire Old Testament to attempt to find other passages which might have undergone such an interpretative process. Still more hazardous would be the attempt to give adequate consideration to all those places where textual difficulties have been explained (sometimes, one is tempted to say, have been created!) by the isolation of anti-Samaritan glosses. The snags here are obviously twofold: in the first place, it will be rare to achieve any general measure of agreement that a particular passage represents a gloss at all; secondly, if the presence of a gloss be agreed upon, then it will not necessarily be accepted that its intention was anti-Samaritan. In these circumstances, all that can appropriately be done here is to note the fact that a number of such alleged glosses have been detected, and to give one example by way of illustration. At Judges 5:14 most modern translations (RSV, NEB, Jerusalem Bible) follow the LXX and find in the first part of this verse a reference to the support given by Ephraimites in the battle against Sisera. The Hebrew text, however, is significantly different. A literal translation would run: From Ephraim their root was in Amalek. The suggestion has been made that this unexpected reference to Amalek is the result of the introduction of a single letter into the consonantal text (*b'mlq* for *b'mq*); that Amalek was the traditional enemy of Israel, association with whom would be a deadly insult; and that in this way polemic against the Samaritans as the heirs of Ephraim could be introduced into the Hebrew text at a point after the translation of the LXX. Such a theory, as will be seen, is extremely ingenious, but no one would maintain that it is the only way of accounting for the evidence—some interpreters would accept the Massoretic text as being the more difficult reading, while others might see a corruption explicable in some different way—and this ambiguity is regularly found where anti-Samaritan glosses have been detected. For that reason, while they must be borne in mind as a possible indication of Jewish feelings at a later period in the development of the Old Testament tradition, no further detailed attention can be paid to that aspect of the subject here.[164]

## Summary and Conclusion

No attempt has been made to examine either every passage in the Old Testament which has been held to have direct or indirect reference to the Samaritans, or every suggestion by modern scholars concerning the use of the Old Testament to illustrate Samaritan origins. What has been attempted is some consideration of those passages which have most commonly been seen as relevant, and of what may be hoped to be a representative selection of modern views. The picture that has emerged is in general a negative one, in the sense that none of the passages commonly held to illustrate Samaritanism, or to explain the schism which is thought to have brought it into being, can in fact be held to do so. The apparent testimony of 2 Kings 17 to an eighth-century schism is shown by other biblical passages, as well as by extra-biblical evidence, to have had other original aims, and this is borne out by a closer examination of that chapter itself. The attempts made by modern scholars, some of which have been noted briefly above, to postulate a schism arising because of the exile to Babylon, or in the time of Haggai and Zechariah, or in that of Nehemiah or of Ezra—none of these, when examined more carefully, prove to be supported by the internal evidence of the Old Testament itself, even before we start our consideration of the Samaritanism of a later age, or of the testimony of Samaritan traditions, and discover the difficulty of reconciling these with any of these hypo-

[164] For a consideration of a number of passages which might be understood in this way, see R. Tournay, 'Quelques Relectures Bibliques anti-Samaritaines', *RB*, 71, 1964, pp. 504–39.

theses. It seems most improbable, therefore, that we may rightly speak of any dramatic schism having taken place within the period of the Old Testament itself. Even the evidence concerning the purpose of the Chronicler, which in some ways may be regarded as the most positive so far considered, is best taken as pointing not simply to anti-Samaritan polemic, but to a wider intention of upholding the claims of Jerusalem against those of all rivals; and of such rival claims that of the Samaritans on Mount Gerizim was not necessarily the only one.

Indirectly however, the Old Testament evidence is of value in two ways. First, it is clear that tension between North and South in Israel goes back to a very early date. Such tension is a recurrent theme even in the period of the United Monarchy, and probably goes back at least to the time of the Judges. It is not our purpose here to explore its origins, but it is clear that there is some link between this tension and that which later developed between Jews and Samaritans. It would be wrong to identify them, and suppose that the Samaritans can simply be identified as a continuation of the old Northern kingdom—as we shall see, there is much in Samaritan tradition that militates against that—but it would be equally wrong to deny all connection and continuity.

Secondly, and arising out of the point just noted about the purpose of the Chronicler, the Old Testament evidence is also significant for the way that it highlights particular areas as potential matters of tension. In the end of the Old Testament period, such matters as the place of Jerusalem *vis-à-vis* the claims of other holy places, the exercise of true priesthood, and the attitude to be taken to the sacral traditions of Israel and their interpretation for changing circumstances—these were the issues that were of great moment for Israel's self-identification. Though there were other differences between Jews and Samaritans, these were the areas in which the division between them was deepest.

# 3

# The Later Jewish Literary Evidence

## The Apocrypha

We have seen that the witness of the Old Testament to the establishment of the Samaritan community is never more than ambiguous. No such uncertainties attach to a number of passages in the Apocrypha. We may for the moment anticipate later conclusions by stating that it is clear that during the third and second centuries B.C. a community which we may properly describe as Samaritan was living at Shechem, with its sanctuary on Mount Gerizim, and that this community is the subject of a number of references in the Old Testament Apocrypha.

The first such passage, to which reference has already been made, is found in Ecclesiasticus 50:25f. It deserves to be quoted in full, both because it is the earliest certain reference to the Samaritans, and also because of the issues which arise with regard to the translation.

> With two nations my soul is vexed,
> and the third is no nation:
> Those who live on Mount Seir, and the Philistines,
> and the foolish people that dwell in Shechem.

This is the RSV translation, which is based on the Greek, and follows it by translating ἔθνος in lines 1 and 2 as 'nation' and λαός in line 4 as 'people'. The Hebrew text of Ecclesiasticus, long lost and now substantially recovered, has a different word-usage, with goyim/goy in lines 1 and 4, and ʿam in line 2. Whether this difference is a significant one is a matter which will have to be considered after an examination of the general setting of the passage.

It is probably beyond dispute that the third group here referred to are the Samaritans, and very many scholars would agree that this is at least the first clear reference to them in Jewish writings. Certain points are nevertheless still obscure, and as a result there are limits to the value of the passage as evidence for Samaritan developments. First, the position of this passage in the epilogue to Ecclesiasticus has raised doubts in the minds of some scholars[1] whether or not it should be taken as part of the basic text of the work, which seems from the Prologue to be dated c. 180 B.C. Certainty in this matter is impossible, but despite the somewhat curious juxtaposition of this passage between the eulogy of the high-priest Simon (50:1-24) and the colophon in 50:27-9 (the Psalm-like passage in 51 clearly standing somewhat apart), neither the Hebrew nor the Greek text suggests that any displacement has occurred here, and so it may perhaps best be understood as part of the original, possibly being placed so as to draw a contrast between the glories of Simon and the wickedness of those here condemned.

This question of the significance of the context of our passage leads into consideration of the second difficulty which it presents: clarification of the immediate occasion and nature of the enmity here depicted. It is now generally agreed that the high-priest whose praises are sung in 50:1-24 was Simon II, known as Simon the Just—the use of this title by Josephus for Simon I being generally regarded as an error—who was high-priest at the end of the third century B.C. Rabbinic tradition associated Simon the Just with an episode concerning Samaritan hostility to the Jerusalem Temple. The Samaritans asked permission of Alexander the Great to destroy the Jerusalem Temple; they were permitted to do so by Alexander, but were beaten off by the inhabitants of Jerusalem. The high-priest Simon, dressed in white, went to meet Alexander, who knelt before him as the one whose image he had seen before going into battle. Simon then told Alexander how the Samaritans had deceived him. 'Thereupon Alexander said, "They are herewith given into your hands." The Jews then pierced the heels of

[1] E.g. W. O. E. Oesterley, in R. H. Charles, *Apocrypha and Pseudepigrapha of the Old Testament* (Oxford, 1912), I, p. 511.

the Cuthim and tied them to the tails of their horses and dragged them over thorns and briers until they came to Mount Gerizim. And when they came to Mount Gerizim, they ploughed it under and sowed it with vetch, just as the Cuthim had intended to do with our temple.'[2] The story is of course of interest for the light that it sheds on Jewish attitudes to the Samaritans at a date rather later than we have so far reached, but for our present purpose it may be significant because of the link it suggests between Simon and the Samaritans. The story has usually been dismissed as historically worthless because of the introduction of Alexander the Great in an obviously anachronistic way, but Purvis has suggested that the story may originally have been told, not about Alexander at all, but about Antiochus the Great, the Seleucid ruler contemporary with Simon.[3] Purvis draws attention to a passage in Josephus: 'At this time the Samaritans, who were flourishing, did much mischief to the Jews by laying waste their land and carrying off slaves; and this happened in the high-priesthood of Onias' (*Ant.*, XII, 156). Onias II was Simon's father, but since this episode also is placed in the reign of Antiochus the Great, it is possible that this might be linked with the other story. Purvis suggests that such incidents may provide the background for the hostility shown in Ecclesiasticus. 'In fact, they fit into the general political situation of that time very well, and indicate that the Samaritans were opposed to the political policies of the Jerusalem high priest.'[4]

In general terms a reconstruction along these lines may well be right, for as we shall see subsequently tension over the priesthood was a major issue dividing Jews from Samaritans. At the same time, we may observe certain difficulties which may warn against supposing that Purvis' reconstruction should be followed too closely. There is first the general point that the rabbinic story contains certain legendary features, and it is only a shrewd guess

[2] This text is found in the scholion to the rabbinic work *Megillath Ta'anith* and the translation here given is that found in the Loeb *Josephus*, Vol. VI, Appendix C, pp. 516–18.

[3] Purvis, 'Ben Sira and the Foolish People of Shechem', *JNES*, 24, 1965, pp. 88–94, reprinted as an appendix to his *The Samaritan Pentateuch and the Origin of the Samaritan Sect*.

[4] Art. cit. (p. 127 in *The Samaritan Pentateuch . . .*)

which links it with Antiochus at all—in the tradition as it has been handed down it is firmly linked with Alexander the Great. Secondly, the story in Josephus is unusual in that it ascribes the attack on Judah to 'Samarians' (Σαμαρεις; the Loeb edition gives the alternative translation in a footnote), and this is not one of Josephus' usual terms for the Samaritans. It might be that the inhabitants of Samaria rather than of Shechem are here involved. Finally, such a reconstruction leaves unexplained the fact that the Samaritans, pictured in this episode as opposed to the Syrian ruler, were found a generation later allegedly supporting Antiochus Epiphanes, as will be seen when we turn to 2 Maccabees 6. No doubt the political situation was volatile; but it seems just as likely that any tradition hostile to the Samaritans could be used, regardless of consistency, and for that reason any exact historical reconstruction becomes very problematic.

The last question to be asked in this connection is a more general one; granted the fact that Ecclesiasticus gives clear evidence of anti-Samaritan feeling, and that the passage under consideration is deliberately placed next to the eulogy of Simon, what facet of Judaism is here represented? No precise answer to this question seems possible, just because our knowledge of Judaism is insufficient—to categorize the work in terms of 'Sadduceeism' or 'Pharisaism', as is sometimes done, is to impose misleadingly narrow categories. There is nothing else in the traditions of Judaism which shares the combination of veneration for the Temple and its priesthood with a place in the wisdom, scribal tradition that is characteristic of Ecclesiasticus. All we can say is that we have an indication of hostility between the Samaritans and a Jewish group, probably Jerusalemite, and showing some links with later Sadduceeism, but otherwise not precisely placeable within our knowledge of the spectrum of Judaism.

There remain two textual points which arise from the particular terms used in 50:25f. First, the terminology of the Hebrew, which is found also in the Vulgate though not the Greek, seems to imply a distinction between the two nations, Seir and Philistia, and 'the foolish people that dwell in Shechem' which is 'no nation'. The difficulty arises from the fact that in the Old Testament the two terms used, *goy* and *'am*, overlap in meaning and usage, whereas increasingly in post-biblical Judaism *'am* is reserved for

Israel, and the *goyim* become the unbelievers.[5] But the correct
classification of this passage is very hazardous: on the one hand it
could be grouped with a number of Old Testament poetic or
wisdom texts, where the two terms occur in synonymous parallelism
(e.g. Ps. 106:4f.); on the other hand it could be argued that in
Ecclesiasticus we have already reached the stage at which *goy*
meant specifically the non-Jew. All that can be said, therefore,
is that 'those who live on Mount Seir', that is the Edomites, and
the Philistines, are named here as having been traditional enemies
of Israel through much of her history. In the case of the Philistines
this must have been drawn from tradition rather than representing
current reality, unless with Oesterley we see here a reference to
the process of Hellenization that was then taking place in the old
Philistine area.[6] Possibly the way in which the Samaritans are
described is intended to be a more specific repudiation, that they
claim to be an integral part of the *'am*, the chosen people, but are
held by Ben-Sirach to be no more than an ignorant or foolish
(Heb: *nābāl*) *goy*.

The second textual point may be dealt with more summarily.
It has so far been assumed that the reading of the Hebrew and
Vulgate is correct in referring to the mountain of Seir. It should
be noted that the Greek has 'mountain of Samaria' (cf. AV, RV).
If this were original, it would be a further reference to the Samaritans, but it seems much more probable that the threefold condemnation of Seir, Philistia and Shechem is original, and that
the reference to the mountain of Samaria is a textual corruption
in the Greek, either through a scribal error, or through an inten-
tional increase of anti-Samaritan material. No new principle
appears to be involved thereby.

Ecclesiasticus affords us clear evidence of anti-Samaritan
polemic; another passage from the Apocrypha gives further
indications of the same tendency. In 2 Maccabees 6 an account is
given of the activities of Antiochus Epiphanes in Palestine. First
he forced the Jews 'to forsake the laws of their fathers and to cease
to live by the laws of God, and also to pollute the temple in Jerusalem and to call it the temple of Olympian Zeus, and to call the

[5] A. Cody, 'When is the Chosen People called a *goy*?', *VT*, XIV, 1964,
pp. 1–6.
[6] Oesterley, in Charles, op. cit., p. 511.

one in Gerizim the temple of Zeus the Friend of Strangers, as did the people who dwelt in that place' (2 Macc. 6:1–2).[7] Here once again we have a slighting reference to the Samaritans, with the implication that they welcomed the Hellenizing policy which was resisted by all true Jews; here once again there is difficulty in assessing the precise origin and character of this attack. 2 Maccabees is notoriously difficult for the critical problems that it presents, of date and purpose, of the group from which it originates, and of the relation between the 'epitomist', as he is usually described, and Jason of Cyrene, whose otherwise unknown history is being epitomized (2:23). It should also be borne in mind that there is another reference to Gerizim in the book, at 5:23, where it is stated that among the governors appointed by Antiochus was one named Andronicus at Gerizim. The thrust of this passage is against the injustices perpetrated by the governors, and there is no hostility in the reference to the community at Gerizim. It has already been noted[8] that no distinctive name is here given to that community, and they are here treated as being within the totality of Israel. A very different impression is created by Josephus' version of what seem to be the same events, as we shall note when we consider the relevant passage in *Antiquities* XII.

Perhaps the best way to approach an understanding of the context which explains these references in 2 Maccabees is in terms of the known historical development in the second century B.C., since it seems to throw some light on the literary situation. It is generally agreed that John Hyrcanus destroyed the Samaritan Temple in 128 and eventually brought to an end the occupation of Shechem itself.[9] Though the period covered by 2 Maccabees ends before the time of John Hyrcanus, and some would regard it as probable that the book was already composed by then,[10] it seems likely that the book represents a similar point of view to that which was carried into action by Hyrcanus. An already existing tension between the communities of Jersualem and Shechem was

[7] For a discussion of the meaning of this last phrase, see Kippenberg, op. cit., p. 76, note 79.

[8] Above, p. 10.

[9] See below, pp. 113f.

[10] So, for example, N. J. McEleney, in *The Jerome Bible Commentary*, I, p. 463.

intensified by different attitudes to the policy of Hellenization which the Seleucid rulers were attempting to impose. Probably the Samaritans did not regard it with the same bitter resentment and resistance as characterized those groups of Jews whose literary memorial has come down to us, and through whose eyes we almost inevitably view these events. In fact, of course, there were deeper divisions among the Jews than might at first seem apparent,[11] and no doubt part of the purpose of the books that have come down to us was to explain why the policy of resistance was the only proper attitude for the people of God. Jerusalem and Gerizim were the two main centres of concern for the Seleucid authorities (2 Macc. 5:22f.), and the Jerusalem Jews came to regard as outright treachery the failure of the Samaritans to pursue the same policy of active resistance as they themselves engaged in. Such a failure justified the Jews, when they had power and opportunity, in destroying the Gerizim temple and so achieving vengeance on the Samaritans. 2 Maccabees, therefore, is concerned not only with exposing the wickedness of the Hellenizers but also with attacking those who failed to resist with sufficient vigour, with the clear implication that they would fall under the same condemnation. Part of the clearly apologetic character of the book is thus explained if it is taken as a literary counterpart of the policy translated into action by John Hyrcanus.

Only one other work in the Apocrypha appears to have any direct reference to the Samaritans—the book of Judith. This work was probably also composed in the second century B.C., though it is much more difficult to date than the other works considered, because its tale is set in the long-distant past, and there are few indications of the contemporary situation. It is commonly assumed, however, that a situation not dissimilar to that underlying the books of Maccabees is involved—the threat of a foreign enemy against Israel which must be resisted by the united efforts of all Israelites in loyal and determined resistance. In two places there are slighting references to the Samaritans: in chapter 5, Achior, the Ammonite leader, who is portrayed very sympathetically, outlines to the enemy general, Holofernes, the great events of

---

[11] On this, see Purvis, op. cit., pp. 127ff.; Reicke, op. cit., pp. 49ff. This division within the Jewish community is also implicit in such passages as 1 Maccabees 6:21ff.

Israel's past, culminating in the entry into the promised land, to which their God had now brought them back after a further exile by way of punishment. In the description of the entry there is a characteristic list of the peoples driven out before them: 'the Canaanites and the Perizzites and the Jebusites and the Shechemites and all the Gergesites' (v. 16). Four of these names are familiar as regularly occurring in the Old Testament lists of such victims; but the Shechemites are never found elsewhere in such a list, and this seems clearly to be a reference to the Samaritans, treated as an enemy of the true Israel. Again, in Judith's prayer in c. 9 she chooses as an example of heroism from the past the vengeance of Simeon on the Shechemites as described in Genesis 34. As we shall see in other anti-Samaritan writings[12] this action came to be referred to without any of the opprobrium attached to it in other Old Testament passages (cf. Gen. 49:5–7). Here again, then, the Shechemites are taken as the enemies of the people, and it is natural to suppose that the real point of this reference was to the contemporary inhabitants of Shechem.

Thus far, these are slighting references to the Samaritans of the kind we have found in the other apocryphal writings. Certain difficulties do, however, arise in assessing the attitude of the book to the Samaritans. The particular problem concerns the identification of Bethulia, the home of Judith and the centre of the action in the book, but not known from any other source. It was suggested by Torrey more than seventy years ago that Bethulia should be identified with Shechem,[13] both on the grounds of its geographical situation, and on the basis of the form of the word, which Torrey identified as deriving from *bēt 'elōah*, house of God. Among more recent scholars many have accepted Torrey's view, sometimes with hesitation; others have rejected it, and preferred to see in Bethulia a city of the author's imagination, conveniently placed as the locus for the great battle, but not precisely corresponding to any actual city.[14] If the latter view is correct, then the fact of

---

[12] Below, pp. 91f.

[13] Torrey, 'The Site of Bethulia', *JAOS* XX, 1, 1899, pp. 160–72.

[14] Among those who have followed Torrey may be mentioned A. E. Cowley, in Charles, *Apocrypha and Pseudepigrapha*, and P. Winter, in *IDB*, II, p. 1025; among those who have rejected the identification is Kippenberg, op. cit., p. 88.

Samaritans living in the area need not matter—the world of the author would not be the empirical world of his own day, and, as one writer who rejects the suggested identification puts it, 'the author conveniently ignores the ancient enmity between the Israelites and the Samaritans'.[15] Those who accept the identification have sometimes supposed that the use of a pseudonym for Shechem was brought about by hostility to the Samaritans,[16] or, alternatively and less probably, taken this identification, together with the omission of the Samaritans from the contemporary enemies of Israel, as an indication that 'one of the aims of the writer may have been to plead with the Samaritans to make common cause against pagan enemies'.[17] This last suggestion scarcely seems likely in view of the anti-Samaritan tone elsewhere in the book, and it seems most likely that the identification of the city with Shechem should not be pressed. (An alternative view, ingenious but not entirely convincing, is to suppose that 5:16 refers to the expulsion of the original heathen (Canaanite) inhabitants of Shechem, and is therefore intended as a friendly gesture towards the contemporary Samaritans.) On the whole, however, it seems most satisfactory to suppose that the book reflects the antagonism towards the Samaritans that was apparently becoming widespread in the second century B.C., without any implication that anti-Samaritanism was its main purpose.

It is likely, then, that all the three apocryphal writings that have been considered come from approximately the same period; that they all reflect what in general may be called a 'Jerusalemite' view without attempting to place any of them more precisely within the overall picture of Judaism; and that all three see one of the issues of their day as being the hostility between Jerusalem and Shechem which we have been outlining. The Samaritans are not yet described by names which would imply that they are no part of Israel, yet their attitude is regarded as being likely to fragment the chosen people, and to lead to its weakening in the face of its enemies. It will emerge from the later parts of this study that this attitude, of hostility still for the moment within the family, fits in well with the total picture available to us.

[15] D. R. Dumm, in *The Jerome Bible Commentary*, I, p. 625.
[16] So Cowley, op. cit., I, p. 251.
[17] Winter, art. cit., p. 1025.

## The Pseudepigrapha

It is conventional and convenient to pass from the Apocrypha to the Pseudepigrapha, even though the dates involved may mean that we pass to a period a good deal later than we have so far been considering and may subsequently have to retrace our steps. There are not in fact many references to the Samaritans in the body of writings usually known as the Pseudepigrapha.

The most important such passage is the reference to Shechem in the Testament of Levi, chapters 5 to 7. The question of the origin of the Testaments of the Twelve Patriarchs continues to be vigorously debated, and it is obviously not appropriate here to enter into that discussion. All that can usefully be said is that the discovery of parts of the Testament of Levi in Caves 1 and 4 at Qumran has suggested to many the likelihood of a pre-Christian origin for the work, though other scholars continue to hold that the Testaments are basically a Christian work.[18]

We cannot therefore be confident about the date of the passage in the Testament of Levi, but that it has a Samaritan reference will scarcely be disputed. Levi outlines the events of Genesis 34— and here unlike Judith 9 there is a reference to the disapproval of Jacob, mentioned in Genesis 34:30 and 49:5-7—and then lists further evils committed by the Shechemites, no parallel to which is found in Genesis: 'they sought to do to Sarah and Rebecca as they had done to Dinah our sister. And they persecuted Abraham our father when he was a stranger, and they vexed his flocks when they were big with young; and Eblaen, who was born in his house, they most shamefully handled. And thus they did to all strangers, taking away their wives by force, and they banished them' (Test. Levi 6:8-10). This is said to have brought God's judgement upon the Shechemites, and in the following chapter the point is stressed by a still more specific allusion to the Samaritans: 'For from this day forward shall Shechem be called a city of imbeciles' (7:2), a judgement strongly reminiscent of Ecclesiasticus

---

[18] A summary of views may be found in Eissfeldt, op. cit., pp. 633ff. See also the article by M. de Jonge, 'Christian Influence in the Testaments of the Twelve Patriarchs', *Novum Testamentum*, IV, 1960, pp. 182–235. The debate is a continuing one.

50:26, and very different from the usual Old Testament view of Shechem.

Another pseudepigraphal work which draws upon the traditions of Genesis in a way which seems clearly to indicate anti-Samaritan feeling is Jubilees. In *c.* 30 an expanded version of Genesis 34 is found; here once again the brothers are praised for their action, the account of the circumcising of the Shechemites being omitted, so that it simply appears that they are killed on account of the rape of Dinah. Only in the doubtful reading of v. 25 is there a suggestion of condemnation; the surviving versions have 'Jacob spoke to them because they put the city to the sword, for he feared those who dwelt in the land', but Charles argued that some verb such as 'reproached' must have been in the original to account for the total context.[19] Otherwise Simeon and Levi are praised, and much of the chapter is given over to a warning of the dangers of any contact between Israel and the Shechemites. 'And thus let it not be done again from henceforth that a daughter of Israel be defiled; for judgement is ordained in heaven against them that they should destroy with the sword all the men of the Shechemites because they had wrought shame in Israel. And the Lord delivered them into the hands of the sons of Jacob that they might exterminate them with the sword and execute judgement upon them, and that it might not thus again be done in Israel that a virgin of Israel should be defiled. . . . And on the day when the sons of Jacob slew Shechem a writing was recorded in their favour in heaven that they had executed righteousness and uprightness and vengeance on the sinners, and it was written for a blessing' (vv. 5, 6, 23).

Two themes over and above those already noted elsewhere seem to be present in this section of Jubilees. There may be the beginnings of a warning against any inter-marriage with the Samaritans, a theme which frequently recurs at a later period, in the rabbinic writings; and the stress on, and justification of, the destruction of Shechem suggests some connection with John Hyrcanus' destroying of the city in 128, so that a justification for that action may also be found here, and this would fit in with the usual dating of Jubilees, at the end of the second century B.C.[20] The discovery

---

[19] Charles, in *Apocrypha and Pseudepigrapha*, II, p. 59.
[20] Kippenberg, op. cit., pp. 89f.

of fragments of Jubilees at Qumran suggests that it may have originated with the Qumran community or a similar group, and we are thus further helped to see something of the divisions and variety within Judaism in the last centuries B.C.

It is not the intention of this present study to attempt to discover every allusion to Samaritanism in the literature of Judaism. Such an enterprise would indeed be a daunting one. In general, however, the impression gained is that the number of such references in the Pseudepigrapha is not large, and that the only allusions that are beyond serious dispute are those already noted. This apparent lack of references may, of course, be illusory, and it might be that some of the cryptic and veiled stories of enemies in the apocalyptic writings are in fact intended to refer to the Samaritans. On the whole this seems unlikely; greater foreign threats were the real danger to the Jewish people, and it was for deliverance from such enemies that the apocalyptists prayed. In this way we are enabled to see that, while Samaritanism had an important, and in some views a dangerous, role in the Jewish struggles of the last centuries B.C., and the beginning of the Christian era, anti-Samaritan feeling was by no means the dominant motif in the writings of that time.

*Josephus*

Sufficient reference has already been made to the *Antiquities* of Josephus to show the importance of his work, not only for the amount of information it provides about Samaritanism, but also for the way in which it has affected modern reconstructions. In view of the use made by the writers of the Testament of Levi and Jubilees of the story in Genesis 34, it is interesting to notice that Josephus' version of it shares a number of the same features: no reference is made to the circumcision of the Shechemites, nor to Jacob's condemnation of the action. Instead, God is seen giving a word of encouragement to Jacob. The tradition is clearly shaped in the same quarters as influenced Test. Levi and Jubilees, and displays an anti-Samaritan tendency. The absence of any reference to the circumcision of the Shechemites might be motivated by a desire to pass over a feature which, in the biblical story, reflects discredit on Simeon and Levi, but it is also possible to see here a suggestion that the Samaritans were outside the chosen people, with circumcision being taken as the seal of the covenant.

In the later books of the *Antiquities* there are, of course, many direct references to the Samaritans, and some attention must be paid to these since cumulatively they are our largest source of information about early Samaritanism. We have already noted some of the features of Josephus' version of the story in 2 Kings 17,[21] with the various names he uses for the Samaritans, and the imputation of syncretistic worship. Of particular importance as a recurring theme in Josephus is his closing comment, which ends Book IX: 'They alter their attitude according to circumstance and, when they see the Jews prospering, call them their kinsmen, on the ground that they are descended from Joseph and are related to them through their origin from him, but, when they see the Jews in trouble, they say that they have nothing whatsoever in common with them nor do these have any claims of friendship or race, and they declare themselves to be aliens of another race. Now concerning these people we shall have something to say in a more fitting place' (*Ant.* IX, 291). This ambivalent attitude does in fact appear to have been characteristic of relations between the two communities at the beginning of the Christian era, though not, as Josephus states, practised on the Samaritan side only.

The passages which claim particular attention are, however, in Book XI, which deals with the period from the beginning of the reign of Cyrus to the death of Alexander the Great, and this was clearly the 'more fitting place' that Josephus had in mind to set out his view of the Samaritans more fully. We have already observed how Josephus' version of the story in Ezra 4 makes the opposition to the Jews specifically Samaritan [22] in both of the two accounts which he gives of the episode (*Ant.* XI, 19ff. and 84ff.). It is also noteworthy that Josephus, following in a tradition which goes back to the Chronicler, consistently speaks of the favour shown to the Jews by the Persian emperors, and for Josephus this is often at the expense of the Samaritans (*Ant.* XI, 61  114ff.). But the particular interest in Bk. XI is Josephus' account of the building of the Temple on Mount Gerizim, the first extensive section of the *Antiquities* which lacks an Old Testament parallel. It is a story

[21] Above, pp. 10, 16.          [22] Above, p. 67.

whose reliability and significance have been very variously assessed. Though it is one of the best known of the stories in Josephus which lack a scriptural parallel, it is perhaps helpful to set the story out briefly before commenting upon it.[23]

The high-priest Joannes (perhaps to be identified with the Jonathan of Neh. 12:11) murdered his brother Jesus, and after the Persian authorities had punished the community for this impiety, Joannes died and was succeeded by his son Jaddua. Jaddua's brother Manasses married Nikaso, the daughter of Sanballat, governor of Samaria, who was 'of the Cuthaean race from whom the Samaritans also are descended'. Manasses was expelled from Jerusalem on account of this marriage, whereupon Sanballat promised that a temple should be built for him upon Mount Gerizim, with the agreement of the Persian king Darius (III). Many other priests who had contracted similar marriages joined Manasses. At this point Alexander the Great entered the scene; his conquests led Sanballat to transfer his allegiance to him, and the Temple was duly built. But when Alexander approached Jerusalem he prostrated himself before the high-priest, as being the representative of the God who had guided him in a vision. The Jews were thereafter treated with great favour, and so the Samaritans, in accordance with the principle already noted, professed themselves to be Jews. On the death of Alexander, the story is brought to an end with the note: 'As for the temple on Mount Gerizim, it remained. And whenever anyone was accused by the people of Jerusalem of eating unclean food or violating the Sabbath or committing any other such sin, he would flee to the Shechemites saying that he had been unjustly expelled.' (Summarized from *Antiquities*, XI, 297–347.)

There are many difficulties in the way of accepting this story as historical. There are elements in it which appear elsewhere in Josephus, and others which have a strongly legendary or apologetic character. The story about Alexander prostrating himself before the high-priest bears marked similarities to the story already quoted in connection with the background to Ecclesiasticus, which appears to have been a popular folk-tale.[24] We find here again the

[23] The names are given in their Greek form except when reference has already been made to them in a different form (e.g. Sanballat).

[24] Above, p. 83.

theme of the Samaritans allying or dissociating themselves, according to the state of favour the Jews were enjoying. We find here also the idea that the Samaritan community was basically composed of renegade Jews—all those who had left or been expelled from Jerusalem because of mixed marriages or violation of the food and Sabbath laws. Finally, the episode of the expulsion of the brother of the high-priest for his marriage to a daughter of Sanballat the governor of Samaria bears a remarkable similarity to the story in Nehemiah, in which Nehemiah expels one of the grandsons of the high-priest for his marriage to a daughter of Sanballat the governor of Samaria (Neh. 13:28).

In view of all these difficulties is there likely to be any historicity in the story? In particular, is it any help to us in establishing when the Temple on Mount Gerizim was built? Rowley examined Josephus' story in considerable detail, and after pointing out historical difficulties as well as the literary points noted above (the impossibly brief time in which the Temple must have been built if Josephus' story were true; the absence of any Manasseh in the list of Samaritan high-priests for the period), concluded that the story was so garbled that 'we have no means of knowing when the Samaritan Temple was built'.[25] More recently there have been some signs of a tendency among scholars to allow a greater measure of credibility to Josephus' account, particularly in view of the discovery of the Samaria papyri at Wadi Daliyeh.[26] As will be seen when the archaeological evidence is considered, this removes one of the objections to the historicity of the Josephus story, by showing that there was indeed more than one governor of Samaria named Sanballat. No one of this name is attested at the time of Alexander, but it is argued that the practice of papponymy, the grandson bearing the name of the grandfather, may have been customary, and that a third Sanballat, the one referred to in Josephus, is not so unlikely as might at first sight appear. Purvis is sufficiently convinced by this evidence to regard it as probable that Josephus' story is basically reliable, rather than an unhistorical midrash, and that we can therefore assume with fair confidence that the Samaritan Temple was built about the time of Alexander.[27]

[25] Rowley, *Sanballat and the Samaritan Temple*, p. 265.
[26] See below, pp. 106f.
[27] Purvis, op. cit., pp. 102–5.

This date for the Temple may indeed be a likely one, but it is difficult to resist the impression that the illogicalities in the Josephus narrative are greater than Purvis allows for. Only one of the difficulties in that story has been eased—the fact that there was more than one governor of Samaria named Sanballat. But even before the discovery of the Samaria papyri this had never been regarded as an insuperable difficulty,[28] and none of the other apparently unhistorical features of the Josephus story have been removed. It therefore seems wisest not to regard it as a source of reliable historical information.[29] Whether any elements in it are true is a more difficult question: a case of the classical dilemma when confronted with a story much of which is unhistorical. Does one reject the whole as a fabrication, or does one seek for those elements in it which may be regarded with greater confidence? This dilemma is as much one of temperament as of methodology, and we may note simply that—whether Josephus had a reliable source or not—it is likely on archaeological grounds that the Gerizim Temple was built at about the date he implies. For the rest, the story has more to tell us of the anti-Samaritan feeling of his own time than of the history of the fourth century B.C.[30]

Among references to the Samaritans in later sections of the *Antiquities*, we may note two passages (XII, 10; XIII, 74-9) which refer to disputes in Egypt between Jews and Samaritans. The stories are extremely similar, and may be duplicate versions of the same set of events; both are placed by Josephus in the second century B.C., the first being linked with the persecution of Antiochus Epiphanes, the second more generally within the reign of Ptolemy VI Philometor (180-145). The incident is significant, because for the first time we see evidence of a widening of the dispute between Jews and Samaritans. As expressed by Josephus, the centre of the quarrel concerns the true temple, and whether that of Jerusalem or that of Shechem was that which was the true

---

[28] Rowley, *Sanballat and the Samaritan Temple*, p. 251.

[29] V. Tcherikover, *Hellenistic Civilisation and the Jews* (Philadelphia, 1961), pp. 42ff., takes a very sceptical view of the story, which is a 'myth worthy not of the historian but of the student of literature'.

[30] On the question of sources within this section of Josephus, see A. Büchler, 'La Relation de Josèphe concernant Alexandre le Grand' *Revue des Etudes Juives*, XXXVI, 1898, pp. 1-36, and the criticisms of Kippenberg, pp. 50-6.

fulfilment of God's commands in the Torah. We may thus see from this episode that certainly by Josephus' own time, and possibly from the second century B.C., the disputes between the two communities had already spread into the diaspora, and that it was apparently the nature of the true sanctuary that was at the heart of these disputes. It may be noted in passing that the description of disputes in these terms scarcely fits with the accounts of the pagan ancestry of the Samaritans found elsewhere in Josephus.

There is only one other passage in Josephus which remains to be considered. (The possibility of linking the section XII, 156 with the background to Ecclesiasticus has already been noted.)[31] We have already observed that in 2 Maccabees 5 an account is given of the establishment by the Seleucid authorities of Andronicus as governor at Gerizim, and that no hostility to the community at Gerizim is there shown; they are pictured as being within the totality of Israel.[32] Josephus' account of these events is very different in tone.

In accordance with what he describes as their usual practice, the Samaritans' reaction to Jewish misfortune at the time of Antiochus Epiphanes is to deny any kinship with them, 'thereby going in accordance with their nature'. Instead they claimed to be colonists from the Medes and Persians (which, says Josephus, is the truth) and call themselves 'the Sidonians in Shechem'. They then wrote to Antiochus, repudiating Sabbath-observance, rejecting any association with the Jews, asking that his ill-treatment of them might stop because it was due to their being wrongly linked with the Jews by the royal officials, and asking for their Temple to be dedicated to Zeus Hellenios; these requests were received with favour by Antiochus, and persecution ceased, and the Temple was dedicated in accordance with their wishes (*Ant.* XII, 257–64).[33]

There has been dispute concerning this incident, and the letters that Josephus has preserved. There are certain features in the letters, such as the use of the correct royal titles, which might suggest that there was an authentic source, dating back to the second century B.C., underlying this correspondence, but it is scarcely possible to doubt that in their present form these letters

[31] Above, pp. 84f.　　[32] Above, pp. 86f.
[33] On the variant readings, 'Zeus Hellenios' and 'Zeus Xenios', see R. Marcus in the Loeb *Josephus*, VII, pp. 134f.

have been worked over either by Josephus himself or by his
source, to fit in with the unfavourable picture that he gives of the
Samaritans. Thus, various attempts to find a credible historical
explanation for the Samaritan self-designation as 'Sidonians' seem
less probable than that this is simply a slighting reference to the
alleged ancestry of the Samaritans. The overall picture is that
Josephus is recording a further stage in the rupture between the
two communities, and he is anxious to show that at every stage
the blame must be placed upon the Samaritans.[34]

We have seen reasons for hesitation in accepting the historicity
of each of Josephus' main stories which deal with the Samaritans,
and yet there is no doubt that on a number of important points he
provides valuable insights into the basic matters at issue between
the communities. The emphasis placed on the rival sanctuaries
and on the disputes as to true priesthood are almost certainly
significant pointers in this respect. Of particular interest, too, is
the ambiguity which Josephus describes in the relations between
Jews and Samaritans, with an attitude now of acceptance, now of
repudiation. Josephus implies that it was only the Samaritans
who reacted in this way; in fact, as we shall see, this attitude seems
to have been characeristic of both groups, and seems to have
persisted well into the Christian era. Because of this, the other
ambiguity found in Josephus is more readily explained; at times
he is anxious to stress (and may even put into the Samaritans'
own mouths) the fact of their foreign origins; at other times they
are part of Israel, even if that part which—according to Josephus—
sat most lightly on the obligations laid upon the covenant community. There is often a feeling that the Samaritans are something
of an embarrassment to Josephus; he cannot repudiate them
entirely, and yet they cannot be accepted as part of that race whose
Antiquities he is setting out to his audience. Such a view, rather
than any extensive source analysis, seems best to explain the
ambivalence of his attitude. In the end Samaritan claims had to be
rejected, and it may well be that—in so far as his work was addressed
to a Jewish context—the repudiation of Samaritanism may have
been one of the purposes of his writing.

[34] Kippenberg, op. cit., pp. 77–80, discusses various features of this
passage, and takes a somewhat more optimistic view of the possibility
of discerning a historical basis to the correspondence.

*Summary and Conclusion*

The Old Testament evidence concerning the Samaritans is, as we have seen, never better than ambiguous and may well be non-existent. When we reach the second century B.C. the various works noted in this section leave no room for doubt that there was a Samaritan community based on Mount Gerizim set over against the Jewish community which looked to Jerusalem. The rivalry between them, affecting as it did both the interpretation of the holy traditions and the claims of different sanctuaries with their priesthoods, went to the heart of Judaism's most sacred beliefs and hence was seen by all those writers whom we have been considering as a real threat to the unity of the people. On their view, the differences thus expressed were more vital than the many other points which Jews and Samaritans had in common.

If the accounts in Josephus of disputes in Egypt in the mid-second century B.C. are to be accepted this rivalry was already one which had spread well beyond the borders of Palestine. The writings we have just been considering recognize this antagonism as a fact, and make little attempt to explain how it came about—with the exception of Josephus, whose story is based on the Old Testament material and which cannot be accepted as it stands as a straightforward account of Samaritan origins. It is therefore appropriate at this point to see if there is evidence of any other kind which will help us to explain those origins. In particular, we must now ask what contribution archaeological investigation can make to our inquiry.

# 4

# The Evidence of Archaeology

A number of the literary references which have been noted thus far have been regarded as being further illuminated by archaeological data, and before we turn to the Samaritans' own self-portrait, it is appropriate to consider the significance of such data. For the most part, of course, it is Palestinian archaeology that is of immediate interest, but before attention is given to the evidence from Samaria and Shechem, the papyri from Elephantine may first claim our attention.

The first significant point to be noted is the very existence of the Elephantine Temple. Before it was discovered at the beginning of this century, it was generally assumed that the law of one sanctuary, as set out in Deuteronomy (12:5ff.), was universally observed. If that had indeed been so, then the building of the Samaritan Temple on Mount Gerizim would have been a major and, one might feel, unforgivable schism within Judaism; the fact of the existence of a Temple at Elephantine, apparently accepted in quite a matter-of-fact way, gave a different complexion to the matter. As we shall see later in this section, it could now be argued that the erection of the Samaritan Temple might not have involved quite such an irrevocable split as was previously thought.

The papyri themselves make no mention of the Samaritans, or of Shechem, but they throw an interesting light on the relation between the authorities in Jerusalem and those in Samaria. Two of the papyri relate to an appeal which the Elephantine Jews evidently felt quite able to address to the two cities jointly. The petition describes the destruction of the Temple at Elephantine and appeals to Bagoas, the governor of Judea, for help. Near the end it states: 'Further we have set out the whole matter in a letter sent in our name to Delaiah and Shelemiah, the sons of Sanballat the governor of Samaria.'[1] Perhaps more significant still is the fact that Bagoas and Delaiah sent a joint reply, which has not survived but is referred to in another papyrus.[2] Bagoas and Delaiah are counterparts, and it is no more accurate to think of Delaiah as a representative Samaritan than it would be to regard Bagoas as a representative Jew. The position of Bagoas in relation to the Jewish religious leaders is uncertain, but it seems probable that he is to be identified with 'Bagoses the general of Artaxerxes' who had laid down punishment for the Jews after the murder of Jesus by his brother the high-priest in Josephus' story (*Ant.* XI, 300)— a further pointer against the historicity of that story, with its setting at the time of Alexander.[3] Bagoas was the imperial representative; and so too were the authorities in Samaria, acting in a way similar to that of Sanballat at an earlier stage. There is no link here with the Samaritans.[4]

This point is relevant also when we turn to the archaeological evidence from Samaria. We have noted already[5] that the association with Samaria appears to be no more than part of the polemic against the Samaritans at a time when Samaria had become a paganized city of the Hellenistic world, and that possibly in the Old Testament (2 Kings 17:29) and certainly on a number of occasions in Josephus this link is deliberately but misleadingly stressed. It may also be recalled that in the story at *Antiquities* XII, 156, Josephus actually speaks of 'Samarians' rather than 'Samaritans' and it is obviously possible that he, or the source he was following, here had a different group in mind.[6] In any case, the attitude of hostility to Samaria went back to much earlier times; it had always been associated in the thought of Judah with an admixture of foreign religion. Samaria was a kind of royal enclave within the Northern kingdom. Concerning its founder, Omri, the biblical tradition is notoriously reticent; but his son Ahab

---

[1] *DOTT*, p. 264. Cf. above, p. 58, for the implications of this section for the position of Sanballat.

[2] *DOTT*, p. 266; *ANET*, p. 492.     [3] Above, pp. 95f.

[4] The state of affairs here revealed argues strongly against the view of Eybers (art. cit.) that the schism had already taken place, but that the settlers in Egypt may have been ignorant of events in Palestine.

[5] Above, p. 9.     [6] Above, p. 85.

was regarded with deep suspicion in at least one tradition preserved in the books of Kings for his marriage to Jezebel and his toleration of her Baal cult (1 Kings 16:29–33; but cf. 1 Kings 21:27–9).[7] It may also be significant to bear in mind that, just as Jerusalem stood somewhat apart from Judah, so it was with Samaria and Israel, the capital forming a distinct political entity within the northern state.[8]

The archaeological evidence from Samaria in the period following the Assyrian conquest is somewhat scanty, though it is known that the city retained an important role as the seat of the Assyrian, and subsequently of the Babylonian and Persian, governors.[9] However sympathetic particular individuals among them may have been to the native inhabitants, they were clearly the representatives of a foreign power. After Alexander's conquest the amount of archaeological evidence is again greater, with the revival of Samaria as a centre of Hellenistic civilization. Its very existence thus became a standing reproach to the stricter members of the Jewish community in Jerusalem, and it is easy to see how it would be an effective insult to associate the Samaritan community with Samaria. But such an association in fact seems to have amounted to no more than the extremely generalized one that the Samaritans represented a northern tradition and Samaria was for long the capital of the Northern kingdom. Samaritan tradition consistently repudiates any connection with Samaria.[10] It has, nevertheless, been argued by some scholars that the changing fortunes of Samaria were important in the establishment of Samaritanism, and this theory will be considered in the context of our treatment of the archaeological evidence from Shechem.

Until shortly before the beginning of the first world war the exact site of the ancient city of Shechem was unknown, though its location in the general area of Nablus (ancient Neapolis) was of course certain. It is now well established, however, that the ancient

---

[7] On Samaria as a royal enclave, see Alt, 'Der Stadtstaat Samaria', *KS*, III, pp. 258–302, and Ackroyd, 'Samaria', in *AOTS*, Oxford, 1967, pp. 343–54.

[8] Alt, 'The Monarchy in the Kingdoms of Israel and Judah', in *Essays in Old Testament History and Religion* (Oxford, 1966), p. 249.

[9] Alt, 'Die Rolle Samarias bei der Entstehung des Judentums', esp. pp. 318–333.

[10] Above, p. 9.

site lies at the modern village of Balatah, and extensive excavations during the last sixty years have confirmed the importance and antiquity of the site, with traces of human settlement dating back to the fourth millennium B.C.[11] The city's importance in the second millennium is illustrated by references in the Egyptian Execration Texts and the Tell el-Amarna Letters, and this importance lasted into the Biblical period. We have already observed how later writers used the story in Genesis 34—undoubtedly an ancient tradition—of contacts with the Shechemites in patriarchal times, and both in the period of settlement (Josh. 24) and in the first attempt to establish kingship in Israel (Jdg. 8:30–9:57) Shechem played a prominent part. It was, of course, at Shechem that 'all Israel' met Rehoboam after the death of Solomon, to consider the terms of his kingship (1 Kings 12), but it was apparently soon abandoned as a capital after the division of the kingdom (1 Kings 12:25). Thereafter its importance declined, and we hear little of it from Old Testament sources during the period of the divided monarchy.[12] Nevertheless archaeological evidence suggests that the site continued in occupation, with several destructions, down to the beginning of the fifth century B.C. The question is obviously raised whether it is possible to correlate this history with the Samaritans' traditions; but the inherent lack of precision in the archaeological evidence, and the uncertainties associated with the Samaritan tradition make this too risky a procedure.

It appears that the site was abandoned for about a century and a half, until a new and vigorous occupation began late in the fourth century (Stratum IV of the excavations). This occupation lasted— not without vicissitudes, for there was a great deal of rebuilding— until late in the second century B.C., the series of coins ending *c.* 110, and at this period 'the last major event at the site was the transfer of a vast amount of earth from the mountain sides to cover over the surrounding Wall and north-west gate so that they could never again be used for fortification.'[13] The traditional site never

---

[11] G. E. Wright, *Shechem* (London, 1965); cf. also the summary article by Wright in *AOTS*, pp. 355–70, on which the archaeological references in the following sentences are based.

[12] One possible exception, Hosea 6.9, has been considered already above, p. 26.

[13] Wright, in *AOTS*, p. 368.

regained its importance, and eventually even the memory of its exact location came to be lost.

There can be no serious doubt of the correctness of Wright's description of this occupational period as 'The City of the Samaritans'.[14] It is a reasonable inference that the site, and in particular its Temple on the adjoining Mount Gerizim, provided a focus of loyalty for its inhabitants set over against the claims of Jerusalem, which were presumably regarded as intolerably exclusive. We may reasonably see during this period a hardening of attitudes between Samaritans and Jews—though we must also bear in mind that a similar hardening of attitudes might well be traceable between, for example, the Qumran covenanters and the Jerusalem Jews during a considerable part of the same period. Once again, that is to say, we need to bear in mind the complexity of the divisions within Judaism, never more acute than at the time when it found itself in a world largely dominated by Hellenistic modes of thought, and when such modes of thought appealed to many within Judaism itself.

Before considering the implications of this archaeological evidence in more detail, it is appropriate briefly to notice that many scholars had previously supposed that a date in the Persian period rather than the Greek period was likely to have seen the rebuilding of the Temple on Mount Gerizim and, as will be seen subsequently, that is not entirely excluded by the latest evidence. Rowley summarized the views of many scholars and concluded that 'we have no means of knowing when the Samaritan Temple was built';[15] in general, however, the tendency seems to have been either to reject the Josephus account altogether, or to suppose that it had wrongly telescoped two separate events—one concerned with Alexander the Great, the other with the building of the Samaritan Temple—and then to suppose that the building of the Temple had taken place earlier than the time of Alexander.[16] Since such a view was largely based on an estimate of the biblical material that found a Samaritan schism as already having taken

[14] Section heading in *AOTS*, p. 367; cf. also *Shechem*, ch. 10: 'The Samaritans at Shechem'.

[15] Rowley, *Sanballat and the Samaritan Temple*, p. 265.

[16] Tcherikover, op. cit., p. 419, following A. Shalit, in *Commentationes in memoriam Johannes Levy*, pp. 252 ff. (inaccessible to me).

place by the time of Nehemiah and Ezra, we need not here consider it further.

Instead, we should turn to the implications of the archaeological evidence. Several questions are raised by it. Why was the site resettled at this particular period after so long a time of abandonment? How do the archaeological data relate to the Samaritan literary traditions? To what extent does the building of a separate Temple imply a definite and irrevocable schism? And, finally, what do we know of the relations of the Samaritans at Shechem with other Jewish groups from this time on?

The first question, concerning the reasons for the reoccupation of the site, has been the subject of two recent suggestions, the first by G. E. Wright, who is followed by Purvis, the second by B. Reicke. Wright, who was in charge of the Shechem excavations from 1956 onwards, finds support for the archaeological data in the Josephus story already discussed concerning the building of the Gerizim Temple at the time of Alexander the Great,[17] and also in other literary evidence. In particular he cites the *History of Alexander* by Quintus Curtius, a Latin writer of the first century A.D., who has a story of the Samaritans burning alive the governor whom Alexander had left in charge of Coele-Syria; and also two writers from a later period still, Eusebius of Caesarea and Syncellus, who state that Alexander settled his own Macedonian troops in Samaria.[18] From these sources, Wright concludes that the reason for the resettlement of the ancient site at Shechem was that Alexander had expelled them from Samaria on account of the outrage they had committed, that city being then resettled with his own veterans. The displaced Samaritans turned to the old and long unoccupied site at Shechem for their settlement.

At this point another piece of archaeological evidence needs to be taken into account, for it has been seen by Wright as giving strong support to his hypothesis. Reference has already briefly been made to the Samaria papyri,[19] and the significance of this

[17] *Antiquities*, XI, 297ff., cf. pp. 94ff. above.

[18] Wright, *Shechem*, pp. 180f., where more detailed references are given; cf. also Wright, 'The Samaritans at Shechem', *HTR*, 55, 1962, pp. 357–66. The literary evidence is also discussed by Tcherikover, op. cit., pp. 45–8.

[19] Above, p. 96.

discovery now arises again. In 1962/3 there were found in a cave in the Wadi Daliyeh, in the remote hills overlooking the Jordan Valley north of Jericho, a number of skeletons and a quantity of papyri, for the most part 'economic documents from Samaria',[20] together with pottery of a type similar to that found in the re-established site at Shechem.

The significance of these papyri has been explored by both Wright and F. M. Cross.[21] One point we have already noted. There is a reference to Sanballat as being the father of the governor of Samaria. On the principle of papponymy, it would have been possible for there to have been a third Sanballat at the time of Alexander, and this would then be the one mentioned by Josephus. Cross's reconstruction suggests that Nehemiah's opponent was the founder of the family, on account of his gentilic, 'the Horonite' (Neh. 2:19), rather than the use of a patronymic; he was succeeded by Delaiah, his son, who is mentioned in the Elephantine papyri; then came the names mentioned in the Samaria papyri, Sanballat and his son Hananiah; and Josephus' Sanballat could then have been next in succession.[22] Such a reconstruction is chronologically possible, though the period from Delaiah to the second Sanballat is a suspiciously long one, but we must of course remember that it is entirely hypothetical. Nor, of course, is there any indication that inter-marriage between the ruling family in Samaria and the Jerusalem high-priestly family took place on more than one occasion, as the Josephus story implies. On the whole, as already indicated, it seems best to regard this discovery as throwing an interesting side-light on the Josephus story rather than in any way corroborating it.

The other aspect of the discovery of the Samaria papyri which is relevant at this point is the identity of the skeletons, of which more than three hundred were found. Wright's suggestion is that they were Samaritans who 'had fled Alexander the Great's punitive expedition against Samaria in 331 B.C. . . . Alexander's

[20] Wright, *Shechem*, p. 181.

[21] Wright, *Shechem*, pp. 180f.; Cross, 'The Discovery of the Samaria Papyri', *BA*, 26, 1963, pp. 110–21; Cross, 'Aspects of Samaritan and Jewish History in late Persian and Hellenistic Times', *HTR*, 59, 1966, pp. 201–11.

[22] Cross, 'Aspects . . .'

troops evidently found the hiding-place of the fugitives from Samaria and suffocated them by building a large fire at the cave's mouth.'[23] This ties in with his whole picture of the events of this period, as suggested by the literary sources already cited.

Such a reconstruction is attractive, though we should note that it contains a number of questionable features. That Samaritan tradition knows nothing of such a story may be regarded as natural, for if it were true it would reflect little credit upon their community. More serious is the late date and not always consistent character of the literary evidence which is adduced to establish this picture. The difficulties in Josephus' account have already been noted, and need not be set out again; but the supporting evidence may be regarded as even more slender. Quintus Curtius' *History* has been dismissed by a classical scholar as 'worthless',[24] while Eusebius' testimony concerning Alexander's resettlement of the city is weakened by the fact that he himself has stated elsewhere that this resettlement was carried out at a later date by Perdiccas, one of Alexander's generals.[25] It is doubtful, too, whether such a reconstruction, drawing together a diversity of literary evidence and combining it with archaeological data, can be regarded as methodologically very satisfactory. Admittedly, it is often necessary to work in this way; it still remains a procedure with very dangerous pitfalls.

There are difficulties of another kind. Stories which link the Samaritans with Samaria may well have a polemical intention, as we noted at the outset, and it is possible that a similar intention is at work in the way in which Josephus links the construction of the Gerizim Temple with the patronage of Alexander, 'to present the detested Samaritan community as the unripe fruit of Hellenistic opportunism', in Reicke's colourful phrase.[26] Finally, doubts may be expressed whether the differences and points at issue between the Samaritans and the Jerusalem Jews were as great in the fourth century as this reconstruction would seem to imply,

[23] Wright, *Shechem*, p. 181.
[24] J. Warrington, in *Everyman's Classical Dictionary* (London, 2nd edn. 1969), p. 175.
[25] For criticism of the literary evidence, see R. Marcus in the Loeb *Josephus*, vol. VI, Appendix C, esp. pp. 520ff.
[26] Reicke, *The New Testament Era*, p. 28.

though here it should be noted that Wright himself gives full weight to continuing links between Samaritans and Jews down to the end of the second century B.C.. and holds that it was no earlier than that period that the final and definitive breach between the two communities took place.[27] For these reasons, it seems wiser to see the developments of this fourth century period as marking a definite change in Judaeo-Samaritan relations rather than commit ourselves to the more precise course of events worked out by Wright.

At this point it becomes necessary to consider a different interpretation of the events of this period put forward by B. Reicke. Starting from the same archaeological data, of a revival at Shechem during the fourth century, he suggests that the re-settlement of Shechem should be placed earlier than the conquests of Alexander, pointing out quite rightly that those views which place all the main developments in the time of his conquests require an improbably speedy development of events. Reicke sees the revival of Shechem as originating in the antagonism of the officials in Samaria and a few aristocrats in Judah towards the centralizing (one might say Zionistic) reforms of Nehemiah, though it was some time after the mission of Nehemiah before the significant developments took place.[28] His assessment of the political situation leads him to the conclusion that the Persian rather than the Hellenistic period was the most likely one for the building of the Samaritan Temple, and he finds yet another way of reconciling the apparently related but divergent traditions in Nehemiah and Josephus by supposing that that the estrangement described in both sources took place c. 380 in the time of Sanballat II (i.e. the Sanballat referred to in the Samaria papyri), and that at that period a group hostile to Jerusalem turned to Shechem and established themselves there, retaining the Torah but no other Scriptures.

This interesting reconstruction has certain obvious strong points, though it also raises a number of fresh difficulties. Indeed, it may be felt that the positive points illustrated are not exactly those which the author set out to establish. However this may be, three points in particular seem to be of especial interest in Reicke's interpretation. First, he lays a good deal of stress on the fact that

[27] Wright, *Shechem*, p. 262, note 25.     [28] Reicke, op. cit., pp. 28f.

the rise of Shechem during the fourth century was as a kind of counterpoise to Jerusalem, an alternative centre of loyalty. This appears to provide a valuable insight into the background of the work of the Chronicler, whether it be considered more likely that his work was written when the revival of Shechem had already taken place, or (perhaps with greater probability) that a main aim of that work was to uphold Jerusalem's claims before the more specific rivalry with Shechem had broken out, for, as we have seen, there is no direct anti-Shechemite polemic in the Chronicler.[29] Secondly, it is proper to recognize, as does Reicke, that it could as well have been the Persian as the Greek period which saw the new developments at Shechem. On this point the archaeological evidence is somewhat ambiguous, since the coins found at the site were apparently entirely from the Greek period, whereas other artifacts appear to be from the Persian period.[30] We are warned once again of the danger of attempting too precise a dating sequence from archaeological evidence. Thirdly, whether or not Reicke's attempt to disentangle the Nehemiah and Josephus story is accepted, his recognition of the tendentious nature of Josephus' writing in regard to the Samaritans is, as our examination of Josephus has shown, an essential point to bear in mind.

Elsewhere, however, Reicke's reconstruction seems to beg certain important questions. When he speaks of the Samaritans 'borrowing' the Torah,[31] this may be no more than an unfortunate way of expressing the matter, for the traditions lying behind the Torah were as much Northern as Southern, and the Torah was itself the inheritance of the whole of Judaism. Much more seriously misleading is Reicke's following statement, 'but, out of caution, the Prophets and Writings were rejected'. At one level, of course, this is simply nonsense: some of the Writings (Daniel, probably Ecclesiastes and Esther) and possibly parts of the prophetic collection (Isa. 24–7? Zech. 9–14?) were not yet in existence to be rejected. That apart, there is a serious over-simplification here. The fact that Judaism eventually came to recognize three divisions in its Canon of Scripture, Law, Prophets and Writings, and that the Samaritans only regarded the first of these as sacred, conceals a complexity of development which is still not entirely

29 Above, pp. 68ff.     30 Wright, *Shechem*, p. 171.
31 Op. cit., p. 29.

resolved, but certainly cannot be dismissed as a Samaritan 'rejection'. We shall need to look further at this question of the Canon when we consider Samaritan traditions.[32]

Another feature of Reicke's reconstruction which seems unsatisfactory is the way in which he follows standard Jewish views of Samaritanism in describing their religious practice as syncretistic. No doubt at a much later date Samaritanism did absorb some features from other religions (Christianity, Islam)—of what religious groups could not the equivalent be said? But the implication underlying the use of the term here is of a Judaism corrupted by the influence of pagan religions; and that is quite misleading. All the indications are that the Samaritans were an intensely conservative group within Judaism, jealously guarding ancient traditions and looking with suspicion on anything that smacked of innovation. To regard such a group as engaged in syncretistic practice seems to be a distortion of the truth.

Neither of these proposed reconstructions of the process which led to the resettlement of Shechem is free from difficulty, therefore, and it may well be that we shall never be able to reach a precise answer to the first of our questions, concerning the significance of a resettlement of Shechem at this particular period of history. The second question concerning the inter-relation of archaeological data and Samaritan literary traditions—can be answered much more briefly. Their Chronicle also tells the story of the rebuilding of the Temple under Alexander, but it is difficult to decide whether this is a genuine independent tradition, or whether it goes back to the same source as one or other of the Jewish stories about Alexander's mode of dealing with the rivalries he found in Palestine.[33] Beyond this the Samaritan tradition does not take us; its prime concern was with the sacred site on Mount Gerizim itself, rather than with the adjoining settlement, and no indication is given concerning reasons for a change at this period.

We must therefore turn to the third of the four questions raised above: to what extent does the building of a separate Temple imply a definite and irrevocable schism? As has been

[32] Below, pp. 152f.
[33] The relevant part of the Samaritan Chronicle II is not yet published. For a survey of the material dealing with this period, see *Encyclopaedia Judaica* 14 (Jerusalem, 1972), p. 730.

indicated briefly already, the older view was that the establishment of such a Temple must have been decisive, because of the
supposed universal acceptance and application of the Deuteronomic law.[34] Such a view took the building of the Temple on Mount
Gerizim as the culmination of a history of developing tension, so
that from this time onwards (whenever the Temple-building was
dated) the total division characteristic of later periods was
established. But it has increasingly come to be recognized that
such a view is an over-simplification, and that the Deuteronomic
requirement was not universally understood and applied in such a
way. As mentioned earlier it was the discovery of the Elephantine
papyri which first brought about the realization that other places
of worship might be accepted; admittedly this was outside
Palestine, but the Jerusalem authorities seem readily to have
accepted its existence, as the papyri show. The existence of other
temples is now well established: at Leontopolis, also in Egypt;
probably at 'Araq-el-Emir in Transjordan, in the complex
associated with the Tobiads;[35] quite possibly also at 'the place
Casiphia' referred to in Ezra 8:17, since it seems likely that some
sort of sanctuary is there referred to, and *māqōm*, place, came
regularly to have this meaning in post-biblical Hebrew.[36] All these
are outside Palestine, but even in Palestine itself it may well be
that the Qumran covenanters had some form of sanctuary. All this
tends to show that the Deuteronomic requirement was interpreted
less strictly than might have been supposed. Perhaps here again
the viewpoint of the Chronicler, with its great emphasis on
Zion, has too readily been taken as the accepted standard of
orthodoxy.

In the light of this variety of practice, it may well be that the
existence of another temple, on Mount Gerizim, would not have
involved so radical a break as might at first sight appear. Rowley,
indeed, suggested that the existence of a Temple on Mount
Gerizim would not have been unwelcome to the Jerusalem
authorities, since northern worshippers would not have been

[34] Cf. above, p. 101.
[35] Cross, 'Aspects . . .', p. 208.
[36] The suggestion was apparently first made by L.E. Browne, 'A Jewish
Sanctuary in Babylonia', *JTS*, 17, 1916, pp. 400f.; cf. also his *Early
Judaism*, pp. 53ff.

readily acceptable there.[37] This must remain a matter of speculation, but it appears more likely than the view of L. E. Browne, who—in yet another proposed re-dating of the book of Ezekiel—saw one of its purposes as an appeal to Jews and Samaritans to come together, 'to sink their differences and unite'; an appeal made necessary by the building of the Temple on Gerizim in 332, a date which Browne claims to work out precisely because of the lapse of 390 years since the fall of Samaria in 722, a period referred in Ezekiel. 4:5![38] Apart from the drastic treatment of the long-suffering book of Ezekiel, we may feel that such precision is unattainable from the type of material available to us.

It would seem, therefore, that the Temple on Mount Gerizim, though obviously important as a symbol of a different focus of loyalty to Yahweh from that represented by the Jerusalem Temple, should not be seen as the decisive cause of cleavage between the two communities. It stands, rather, as one among many different emphases which distinguished the Samaritans within the totality of Judaism—different emphases which will occupy a good deal of our attention in the final part of this study.

So to express the matter is already to indicate the nature of our answer to the last question raised by the archaeological evidence: what do we know of Judaeo-Samaritan relations from this time on? There is for the most part insufficient evidence to construct anything like a historical development; but by considering different aspects of Judaism some picture of the characteristic development of Samaritanism in the last centuries B.C. and the beginning of the Christian era may be obtained. Our last question, then, will underlie much of the remainder of this work.

There is, however, one postcript to be added from the archaeological side. Our attention has thus far been concentrated on the re-establishment of the community at Shechem in the fourth century. Some consideration must briefly be given to what is known of the end of this period of occupation, in the second century. Here the literary and archaeological data correspond more closely, and no very acute difficulties appear to be raised.

---

[37] Rowley, *Sanballat and the Samaritan Temple*, p. 268. Purvis, op. cit., pp. 10–12, stresses more strongly the divisive effect of the Temple-building on Gerizim.

[38] Browne, *Ezekiel and Alexander* (London, 1952).

On the literary side, we have Josephus' statement that John Hyrcanus took 'Shechem and Garizein and the Cuthaean nation, which lives near the Temple built after the model of the sanctuary at Jerusalem, which Alexander permitted their governor Sanballat to build for the sake of his son-in-law Manasses, the brother of the high priest Jaddua. . . . Now it was two hundred years later that this temple was laid waste' (*Antiquities*, XIII, 256), As we have seen, this corresponds well with the archaeological picture of complete devastation in the second century,[39] though Wright acknowledges the extreme difficulty of attempting to reconstruct with confidence any picture of the last period of the settlement before this destruction.[40] We know nothing other than the somewhat tendentious stories already noted in 2 Maccabees 6 and Josephus, *Antiquities* XII, 257ff.[41] of the fate of the Shechem community under Antiochus Epiphanes, and archaeology offers no supporting evidence of any kind here. It was only in the reign of John Hyrcanus that the Jewish state was sufficiently strongly established on an independent basis for such action as that which Josephus describes to be feasible. Some scholars regard the destruction of the Temple and that of Shechem itself as forming part of one campaign, in which case the coin evidence shows that Josephus' dates must be wrong, and both events will be put *c.* 108 B.C.;[42] others accept Josephus' dates and suggest that there were two separate campaigns, one in 128 and the other in 108.[43] The Samaritan Chronicle mentions the destruction brought about by John Hyrcanus, but neither the chronology nor the motivation is sufficiently clearly set out to be of any help. We cannot know in detail why John Hyrcanus took the action he did, nor what he hoped to achieve by it; but it is certain that Samaritanism was not extirpated, and early in the Christian era it seems likely that they had a Temple once more.[44]

[39] Above, p. 104.     [40] Wright, *Shechem*, p. 183.

[41] Above, pp. 86f., 98f.

[42] So D. S. Russell, *The Jews from Alexander to Herod* (Oxford, 1967), p. 63.

[43] So Wright, *Shechem*, p. 184.

[44] The evidence concerning the rebuilding of the temple on Mount Gerizim is somewhat ambiguous, but it seems likely that it took place in the second century A.D. See the discussion in Kippenberg, op. cit., pp. 98–113.

It is not possible to summarize the archaeological evidence in the same way as one may hope to be able to do with literary evidence. As this brief outline will have shown, there is much that is susceptible of more than one interpretation. This is important in itself; and it has also helped to draw our attention to the fact, which is surely beyond serious dispute, that a community which we may properly describe as Samaritan was established at Shechem during the third and second centuries. It is to the Samaritans' own traditions that we now turn.

# 5

# Samaritan Traditions

*Introductory*

The revival of interest in Samaritanism has been described on a number of occasions in recent works, and there is no need here to give more than the briefest summary to give perspective to what follows. It is generally agreed that it was the sixteenth-century French Protestant scholar, J. J. Scaliger, who first showed any appreciation of the significance of the Samaritans, both acquiring manuscripts from them and engaging in correspondence with them, and links of this kind continued, along with visits by western scholars to the Samaritans at Shechem, for the next three centuries.[1] In the present century the publication of J. A. Montgomery's Bohlen Lectures in 1907, simply entitled 'The Samaritans' meant that a great deal of information only available in very scattered or inaccessible form was drawn together conveniently and clearly; the worth of Montgomery's study is still considerable, and it was reissued in 1968. The other great work associated particularly with Samaritan studies in the early years of the present century was the editing by Sir Arthur Cowley of great quantities of Samaritan liturgical material; but since this mostly relates to a later period, we shall not here have occasion to make frequent reference to that very important aspect of Samaritanism. There is no need here to mention the more recent studies, since they will be referred to in the course of our discussion.

Among the Samaritan material whose existence has long been known there are a number of Chronicles dealing with the history

[1] See especially M. Gaster, *The Samaritans*, Appendix I, pp. 159–80.

and traditions of the community. Two of these were edited in the last century; the Arabic work known as the 'Samaritan Book of Joshua', edited by Juynboll in 1848, is a mediaeval work, though probably incorporating some much more ancient material; and the Tolidah, in Hebrew, which is mainly concerned with the generations (*tolidot*) of the high-priestly and other Samaritan families, is another mediaeval work first edited by Neubauer in 1869. Estimates of the historical value of these and other more recently published Samaritan works have varied greatly, but, despite the advocacy of M. Gaster in particular, the general tendency has been—probably rightly—to regard it as very unlikely that these late works preserve genuine historical information concerning the biblical period. They may be of value, therefore, as illustrating Samaritan beliefs; we shall not again refer to them in our consideration of the historical developments.

In recent years, however, the position has significantly altered with the recognition that in another of the Samaritan Chronicles a more ancient and probably more reliable source was available, certainly one that deserved to be set alongside the biblical material as a basis for comparison. This is the Sepher Ha-Yamim, or in the enumeration of its editor, J. Macdonald, Chronicle II. (On Macdonald's enumeration, the Samaritan Book of Joshua becomes Chronicle IV, and the Tolidah is Chronicle III. It seems likely that this form of reference will become standard, and it will be followed here.)

We have opportunity, therefore, to consider first the Samaritans' presentation of their own history as set out in Chronicle II; after that we can consider certain distinctive traits of Samaritan belief and practice, and compare them with the appropriate features of Judaism; and then turn to the other great witness to Samaritanism —the Samaritan Pentateuch, By such means we may hope to be able to establish more accurately the relation of Samaritanism to the world of Judaism in the last pre-Christian centuries.

## Chronicle II

The title of this Chronicle is: 'This is the Book of Days, containing the events of the days from the entry of Joshua the son of Nun into the land of Canaan up to the present day.'[2] The work was in fact continued up to the seventeenth century A.D., so that it is at once obvious that it contains a very great variety of types of material, and that its historical value will vary greatly. Two sections have so far been published: the book known as Samaritan Chronicle II, edited by Professor Macdonald, formerly of Leeds and now of Glasgow; and a much briefer section giving the Samaritans' account of Jesus and the early Christians.[3] This latter, though of considerable intrinsic interest, is not related to our present concerns, and references will be to the first part of the work. This covers the period from the entry into the promised land under Joshua to the time of Nebuchadnezzar's capture of Jerusalem. That is to say, the period covered is that of the biblical books of Joshua, Judges, Samuel and Kings, though, as will become apparent, the biblical tradition of the books of Chronicles is on a number of occasions followed in preference to that in Kings. It is hoped that in due course the remaining parts of the Chronicle which deal with the Old Testament period will be published; in the meantime the best available summary of its contents for this period is probably that in the new *Encyclopaedia Judaica*.[4]

Since there has not yet been opportunity for the contents of even the published part of the Chronicle to become generally known, it seems appropriate to summarize its contents and indicate briefly some of its more striking features. Its starting point is natural enough, since the Samaritans have preserved the Pentateuch, and the story of Joshua in all traditions forms the sequel to the Pentateuch. (Though it is of course perfectly correct to speak of the Pentateuch as the Samaritans' only canonical work, this must not be pressed to the point of making too rigid a distinction between canonical and non-canonical. This is a matter to which it will be necessary to return when we are considering the Samaritan Pentateuch.) Joshua's conquest of the land is described in terms substantially identical with that of MT Joshua 1–11; on the other hand, only a few verses of the remainder of the biblical book find

---

[2] Macdonald's edition, p. 75. References will be to the English translation of this work unless otherwise stated.

[3] J. Macdonald and A. J. B. Higgins, 'The Beginnings of Christianity according to the Samaritans', *NTS*, 18, 1971, pp. 54–80.

[4] *Encyclopaedia Judaica* (Jerusalem, 1972). Vol. 14, s.v. 'Samaritans'.

a place in the Samaritan work, save for the section 13:8–14:5, which is included almost verbatim. There are links with Chronicle IV (the Samaritan Book of Joshua), explained by Macdonald on the grounds of its compiler's dependence on Chronicle II,[5] but the two works are quite different. What they have in common is a veneration for Joshua, which is further illustrated by the fact that variants of the Chronicle II Joshua text exist,[6] some of them incorporating more extensive parts of the biblical book. Two points emerge from this: the first, which we have noted already, and to which we shall have to return, is that though in one sense the Joshua material is non-canonical, yet it clearly enjoyed high esteem, and warns us against too precise a division between canonical and non-canonical writings. The second point of interest is that the Samaritan view of history sets it out in terms of divine favour and disfavour, and the entry into the promised land under Joshua marked the climax of the first great epoch of divine favour which had begun with the patriarchs and was to last until the close of the Judges period. It is noteworthy that such a view of world history as being divided into distinctive epochs is characteristic of much Jewish apocalyptic writing (cf. the four world empires of Daniel) and also of the Qumran scrolls and the New Testament. Such links may provide a further pointer to the date of the formative period of Samaritanism.

The correspondence between the biblical book of Judges and the equivalent part of the Samaritan Chronicle is much less close, largely because of more extensive omissions. The biblical books of Joshua and Judges are of approximately equal length, whereas the Samaritan Judges material is only half the length of Joshua, and much of this is fresh material dealing with the Samaritan high-priests. Old Testament scholars generally agree that the book of Judges' chronology is a schematized one, not to be regarded as a precise sequence, and this editorial process has been carried a stage further in the Samaritan version, where a succession of 'kings' is spoken of—the word 'judges' is rarely used—under the effective control of the high priest at Mount Gerizim; the high-priestly dates form the outline structure of Samaritan chronology. Only the prose account of the defeat of Sisera (Jdg. 4) and the résumé of Israel's past history in Jephthah's

[5] Macdonald, op. cit., p. 12.     [6] Macdonald, op. cit., p. 9.

negotiations with the Ammonites (Jdg. 11) are incorporated from
the biblical text, though knowledge of it is shown by several other
brief sections.[7]

It is the end of the Judges period which is of importance for
our present study. As in the biblical text, the last judge is Samson:
'He was the last of the kings of the era of Divine Favour' (Sam.,
Chr. II. Jdg. K, F*). He is said to have carried out mighty exploits
but no details are given, for all the attention at this point centres
on Eli, who is said to have been contemporary with Samson and
to have quarrelled with the high priest Uzzi. After a struggle, Eli
and his followers left Shechem and established themselves at
Shiloh, with a rival high-priesthood descended from Ithamar
rather than from the true Aaronite line through Eleazar. The story
of Eli and Samuel is then developed in such a way as to show that
this was the decisive period of schism within Israel. The remnant
remained true to the genuine high-priestly line and the proper
sanctuary at Shechem, but others were led astray, some following
Eli, some falling still further into wickedness by acting 'according
to the statutes of the gentiles, worshipping alien gods and bowing
down to them' (Sam. Chr. II, 1 Sam. B, B*). The hostility towards
Saul, already apparent in the biblical accounts of his reign, is
developed further by the Samaritan tradition, and he is held
responsible for an 'exile' of the Samaritans from their sanctuary
lasting twenty-two years (Sam. Chr. II, 1 Sam. J).

This then in Samaritan eyes was the decisive point when the
divine favour was withdrawn and the period of divine disfavour
began. The biblical material at this point offers no help; the
transition from Judges to 1 Samuel is a very abrupt one, without
any of the connecting links which the Samaritan Chronicle
supplies, and the relation of Eli and Samuel to any predecessors
they may have had is not at all clear. What is significant is the way
in which there are other indications of dispute concerning the
genealogy of Eli in the period around the turn of the eras. In 2
Esdras 1:2f., Eli is included in the genealogy of Ezra, which
reaches back to Aaron by way of Eleazar. Eli and his son Phinehas
are included in this genealogy, though not in that in Ezra 7:1-5,

---

[7] This may at some points suggest a variant form of the biblical text.
The names of the judges in particular show a number of deviations from
the familiar forms. See Macdonald, op. cit., pp. 23f.

which is largely made up of the same names; and it therefore seems that the subject of a priesthood transmitted through Eli may have been a matter of dispute early in the Christian era. By contrast to the genealogy of 2 Esdras, an account at the end of Josephus, *Antiquities* V (361f.) tells how the high-priesthood had been handed down in the family of Eleazar to the time of Uzzi son of Bukki, that it then passed to Eli, who was of the line of Ithamar, and that it remained with that branch of the family until the time of Solomon, when it reverted to the line of Eleazar. This is of particular interest, not only because it witnesses to the same tradition as the Samaritan Chronicle describes, but also because the Samaritan tradition claims that Uzzi, son of Bahqi, was the true high-priest at this time. (The Josephus account, Bukki, and the Samaritan Chronicle, Bahqí, fairly clearly have different versions of the same name here.)

It is certainly not possible to take the Samaritan account of events as straight history, any more than was the case with 2 Kings 17. Nevertheless, it is of considerable importance for the indications that it gives of the distinctive features of Samaritanism, and the particular concerns which separated the Samaritans from their neighbours. Here, very clearly, the understanding of true priesthood is of great importance, and this is a subject to which we shall have to return in attempting to place Samaritanism within the larger context of the different groups within Judaism in the last pre-Christian centuries.[8]

Two other points may be noted as arising from this story. As has just been said, it would be unwise to treat the Samaritan account as straight history. It would be equally unwise to dismiss it as of no historical value at all. This being so, we have to reckon with a long period of tension between North and South in Israel, within which the Samaritan tradition was one component part— they should not be regarded as 'the North' *tout court*. This provides a further warning against thinking in terms of a schism in the sense of a sudden dramatic event. The second point is that it appears characteristic of both Jewish and Samaritan tradition to push back the origin of their divisions to as early a date as possible. We have already seen that 2 Kings 17 cannot be accepted as an account of the origins of Samaritanism, and it would be equally

[8] See below, esp. pp. 142–4.

unsatisfactory to suppose that the Jews owed their origin to a
schism at the time of Eli when they broke away from the true
Israel.[9] It seems likely that this tendency should be seen as part of
the general process of emphasizing the differences between Samaritans and Jews by claiming that they had been divided from the
earliest times.

When we reach the books of Samuel, much of the biblical
material that is employed is obviously introduced in a polemical
way, as for example in the use of those passages which dwell on
the wickedness of the families of Eli and of Samuel, but it would
be misleading to imply that the Samaritans simply used the biblical
material in a tendentious way; David, for example, is treated
surprisingly sympathetically. Nevertheless, the overall impression
of the Samaritan work is very different. For the Samaritans the
vital chain of high-priests had long been established, and this
provides the chronological basis of their traditions. Further, the
vital division had already taken place within the community with
the schism at the time of Eli. There is therefore nothing to correspond to the dramatic significance which the biblical account gives
to the establishment of the monarchy, the establishment of
Jerusalem, or the division of the monarchy at the death of Solomon.
This last event, which is of such decisive importance for the
biblical books of Kings, with their constant references to the sin
of Jeroboam the son of Nebat, is much less important for the
Samaritan Chronicle. For this reason, incidentally, Macdonald's
method in his edition of the Chronicle in dividing the text according to the Old Testament parallels, though convenient for reference,
is liable to give a misleading impression of the characteristic
tendencies of the Samaritan work itself.

With the division of the kingdom, in which the Samaritans
represent themselves as being unwilling participants in the struggle
between Rehoboam and Jeroboam, the Chronicle gives a picture
of Israel as divided into four. These were: first, the Samaritans

---

[9] I know of no scholar who would accept that such a statement represented the historical facts of the case, though it is interesting to note that
P. Wernberg-Møller, reviewing Kippenberg, 'Garizim und Synagoge'
in *JJS*, 23, 1972, pp. 90ff., states that M. Gaster and Macdonald accept
the historicity of this schism at the time of Eli. This is surely an exaggera-
tion of their views.

themselves, worshipping on Mount Gerizim under the true high-priest, where they were joined by 'some Levites and some from the rest of the tribes . . . a small number'; secondly, the tribe of Judah, 'along with a very large number who followed them from the rest of the tribes' in their worship at Jebis, the name regularly used in this Chronicle for Jerusalem; thirdly, 'those who were in the city of Pir'aton . . . who followed strange gods of the gods of the nations who lived round about the Israelites. . . . The Israelites called them the Sect of Forsakers'; and fourthly, 'the rest of the tribes of Israel who followed Jeroboam', that is to say, the Northern kingdom, whom the Israelites called 'the Rebellious' (Sam. Chr. II, I Kings XII–XXII, E, A*–K*). The identity of the third group is an obvious puzzle; the title 'forsakers' appears to imply a deliberate contrast to the Samaritan self-designation as 'keepers', but precisely who is meant remains in dispute. The name of the city Pir'aton may be the same as the Pirathon referred to as the home of Abdon in Jdg. 12:15, but that verse is not incorporated in the Samaritan Chronicle, and in any case provides no clue as to the reference here. It may well be that not so much a specific community as a reference to widespread apostasy underlies this statement.

The other noteworthy feature in this description is the distinction drawn between the Samaritans and those who followed Jeroboam. The Chronicle shows no sympathy to the Northern kingdom as such; it is several times specified that it was only eight of the tribes who comprised it, as against the ten tribes of the Old Testament tradition. There has sometimes been a tendency to suppose that, since the traditional view of Samaritanism is clearly untenable, the Jew-Samaritan antagonism was no more than the longstanding north-south rivalry. Such a view, like the one it replaced, is over-simplified.

Such hostility towards the Northern kingdom might lead us to expect a sympathetic attitude to Elijah, who was also bitterly opposed to the Northern kings of his day; but he is in fact described in very hostile terms. His claim to the title of prophet was false; he brought about the death of the son of the widow of Zarephath and stole the last of her food; both he and Elisha spoke words which Yahweh did not command, since he did not speak with them at all; and his death, as a vagabond fleeing from Ahab, was an ignominious one—'he fell into the waters of the Jordan and died'. Other stories in which Elijah plays a prominent part according to the Old Testament are either omitted entirely (the contest with the prophets of Baal) or mutilated (Naboth's vineyard, the story ending with Ahab happily in possession).

G. Fohrer has examined the treatment of prophetic figures in the Chronicle and concludes that the Chronicler's theological outlook required that Moses was to be presented as the only true prophet, and that the normative religious figure was the high-priest on Mount Gerizim. All the Old Testament prophets who are mentioned in the Samaritan work are therefore denigrated as being only self-styled prophets, and sometimes it appears that reference to them is deliberately introduced with this in mind. For example, in the account of Jeroboam II's reign is the note: 'In his days appeared Hosea, Joel and Amos. It is said of them throughout all Israel that they were sorcerers' (Sam. Chr. II, II Kings–II Chronicles, F, B*). With Elijah, however, it seems that a particularly damning picture is given, and this may well be because of the veneration accorded to him in some Judaistic and Rabbinic traditions as a second, perhaps even a greater, Moses; the prominence given to Elijah in some New Testament traditions affords a partial parallel.[10]

The next section of the Samaritan Chronicle which is obviously relevant as a basis for comparison with those biblical traditions we have already studied is that dealing with the last days of the Northern kingdom. The intervening years, corresponding to the early chapters of 2 Kings, are dealt with quite briefly, but a fuller, though in places extremely confusing, account is given of the Assyrian advance in the eighth century. In the description of the last days of the Northern kingdom, frequent reminders are given that it was the 'eight tribes' who were involved,[11] and then the fall of Samaria is described; this is based on 2 Kings 17:1–16, with a number of minor changes which emphasize that the sinfulness being punished was that of the eight tribes and of Judah and Benjamin, and consisted in their abandonment of Gerizim as the

[10] G. Fohrer, *Die Israelitischen Propheten in der Samaritanischen Chronik* II, In Memoriam Paul Kahle, *BZAW*, 103, 1968, pp. 129–37.
[11] 'Ten tribes', in Macdonald, p. 176, at II Kings–II Chronicles F, 2 Kings 15.17, is a mistake for 'eight tribes' in the Hebrew text.

right place for worship—an elaboration which is, of course, without parallel in the biblical text. The remainder of 2 Kings 17, including that section which came to be understood as an account of Samaritan origins, not surprisingly finds no place in the Samaritan Chronicle. Instead, it passes to an account of the 'Syro-Ephraimite' invasion of Judah which uses material from 2 Chronicies 28, and is very different from the picture given in 2 Kings or Isaiah. Zichri, who in 2 Chronicles 28:7 is called 'a mighty man of Ephraim', is described here as 'of the community of the Samaritan Israelites . . . zealous for the Lord his God', and the Ephraimite chiefs of v. 12 are also called Samaritans. Characteristically, in view of the rejection of all prophets other than Moses, the favourable notice of the prophet Oded in 2 Chron. 28:9–11 is omitted. The whole section is thus of great interest; in the biblical book, it is remarkable because it is one of the very rare exceptions to the usual anti-northern bias; in the Samaritan account, it is an important illustration of the use of the biblical material so as to build up a favourable picture of the Samaritan community.

It is clear that the Samaritan Chronicler had no inhibitions about using the biblical books of Chronicles, a fact which suggests that the purpose of those books was not understood by him to have been anti-Samaritan, and it is from 2 Chronicles that most of the account of the remaining years of Assyrian pressure is drawn. There are, of course, considerable omissions and variations, which at times lead to major chronological confusion. This is perhaps not surprising in view of the chronological difficulties of this period in the biblical accounts. Thus, the Samaritan Chronicle describes the events of Hezekiah's reign in a way which implies that the exile of the Northern tribes has not yet taken place. We have noted earlier that while the biblical description of the preparation for Hezekiah's passover states that some northerners accepted his invitation and came to Jerusalem (2 Chron. 30:11), in the Samaritan Chronicle 'the eight tribes (not yet exiled!) laughed them to scorn' (Sam. Chr. II, II Kings-II Chron, J, v. 10).[12] By contrast Hezekiah's messengers were received by the Samaritans, and whereas in the biblical account the keeping of the Passover in Jerusalem is seen as the fulfilment of God's promise to Hezekiah, the Samaritans tell the messengers that it is only on Gerizim that

[12] Cf. above, pp. 19f.

the Passover may properly be observed: 'Walk in the right way, by coming to the chosen place Mount Gerizim Bethel to perform the Passover offering here, as the Lord, the God of Israel, commanded' (ib. E*).

2 Chronicles 31 is concerned with Jerusalem and is omitted, but 2 Chronicles 32—rather than 2 Kings or Isaiah—is followed in the account of Sennacherib's invasion of Judah, though in much reduced form and with the favourable references to Hezekiah omitted. At this point considerable confusion is found, which is best illustrated by quoting the first three sections of II Kings–II Chronicles L: 'In the thirty-ninth year of the priestly reign of the High Priest Halel, Manasseh the son of Hezekiah began to reign. This was during the time of Azariah the son of Amaziah king of Judah. Two sons were born to him; the first was called Shear-yashub, and the second Maher-shalal-hir-baz.' There is no obvious reason for this confusion: Azariah was Manasseh's great-great-grandfather; and the two sons named are recognizably those of Isaiah in the Old Testament (with a slight change in the name of the second). We cannot here attempt to explore this further, but we are warned of the secondary character of the Samaritan work.

There follows another section unrepresented in the biblical material. Once again the fall of Samaria and the fate of its inhabitants are described, in terms not directly dependent upon the Old Testament; and then it is told how the Samaritans themselves suffered. They were forced to leave Mount Gerizim for Haran, and after hiding the holy vessels and leaving the book of the law to be guarded by the priests, they went into exile, with the doors of their temple left open behind them as they sang a lament. The names of their leaders are listed, and the event is dated, 3,548 years from creation, 754 years after the entry into the holy land, and 494 years after the hiding away of the holy sanctuary (at the time of Eli). If we relate it to other dates more familiar from Old Testament history, it took place 274 years after the building of Solomon's Temple, and 124 years before the exile from the Southern kingdom. A date close to the traditional one of 722 is thereby achieved, but precision is obviously impossible.[13] It is

---

[13] Macdonald uses the northern exile, 722 B.C., as the 'fix' for the Samaritan chronology (Appendix V, pp. 220–2). It is doubtful whether that chronology can really support the claims for accuracy which he makes.

further stressed that not only the Samaritans but all Israel underwent the same fate at this time: 'This happened to all Israel, to the community of the Samaritan Israelites, to the community of the eight tribes of Israel, and to the community of the Judaeans' (Sam. Chr. II, II Kings–II Chron., L, CC*). There follows a note to the effect that the so-called prophetic words to the people of Judah concerning their safety had been misleading; they were, once again, no true prophets. Isaiah is not mentioned by name, but it appears likely that it is his words which are being compared unfavourably with the genuine salvation which had been wrought through Moses and Aaron.

Another section without an Old Testament parallel follows, in which Pharaoh Senes took other Israelites captive to Egypt. This episode is regarded by Macdonald as a possibly genuine independent tradition, the Pharaoh in question being Sefnakht of the XXIVth dynasty (720–718).[14] This may be so, yet it would be misleading to put much weight on this as an indication of chronological reliability, since an even greater confusion then follows. It is first stated that the Samaritan book of the law was taken to Nineveh, and a tax imposed upon both the Samaritans and the people of Judah, on the payment of which they were allowed to return from their exile, after a period of forty-seven years. The Old Testament knows nothing of this return; and there follows in the Samaritan work the unexpected statement: 'So all Israel came under the dominion of the kings of the Edomites, that is, the kings of Persia. [Thereafter] the rule passed over to the Greeks' (Sam. Chr. II, II Kings–II Chron, M, O*). (The word 'thereafter' is inserted to ease the chronological dilemma; the original, which continues in the simple narrative style with consecutive imperfects, gives no indication of this.) Such a section, coming as it does before the description of Manasseh's reign, is a warning against any confident expectation that it will be possible to reconstruct Samaritan history from this Chronicle. That in no way detracts from the other ways in which it is a valuable witness to Samaritanism.

The contents of the remainder of the published part of the Samaritan Chronicle may be outlined more briefly, since the problems raised are markedly fewer. In the account of the reign of Manasseh, the wording is substantially that of 2 Chron. 33:1–11,

[14] Macdonald, op. cit., p. 185.

but the overall impression given is much closer to the account in 2 Kings 21, for the Samaritan work makes no mention of Manasseh's conversion, as described in the remainder of 2 Chron. 33. This is in line with the general custom in the Samaritan Chronicle, of following the biblical account when it speaks of the wickedness of kings of Judah, but ignoring references to their good behaviour. After Amon's brief reign, the account of Josiah affords a further example of this principle of selection. The Samaritan version simply notes his accession, and his death at the hands of Pharaoh Neco's archers (cf. 2 Chron. 35:20), with no mention of those other events in his reign which are given such prominence in the Old Testement account. The reasons for these omissions are not far to seek: the finding of the law-book was irrelevant to the Samaritans; the purification of the Jerusalem temple-cultus was *ex hypothesi* impossible; and the extension of Josiah's power into the northern territory was contrary to the account already given of the fate of the Samaritans and the other inhabitants. Instead, the only event associated with Josiah's reign is the work of Jeremiah, who is treated as unsympathetically as the other prophets: 'he began to claim for himself that he was a prophet of the Lord, the God of Israel, but many of the people of Judah conspired against him, stoning him to death' (Sam. Chr. II, II Kings–II Chron. N, H*–I*).

The only point that requires particular notice in the remainder of the 'pre-exilic' section of the Samaritan Chronicle is the statement made concerning Jehoiakim that he 'ruled over the people of Judah and over the community of the Samaritan Israelites and over the rest of the tribes' (*ibid*,. K*). This fits in with the idea of the forty-seven-year period of exile, which would now be over. Such a picture scarcely corresponds, however, with the account of Nebuchadnezzar's invasion, which is based on the last chapters of 2 Kings, and makes no mention of the Samaritans save for the notes of the high-priestly succession. Here as elsewhere inconsistencies in the account of the community's history have not been ironed out.

The published part of the Samaritan Chronicle ends with the restoration to favour of Jehoiakim in Babylon. As already noted, however,[15] the work is a continuous one extending far into the

[15] Above, p. 118.

Christian era, so that it is appropriate briefly to note some of the distinctive features of its treatment of the later pre-Christian centuries.[16] In general, the Samaritan work seems largely to be dependent upon the biblical material, and the notorious historical and chronological problems associated with the biblical material for this period mean that the Samaritan accounts are very confused. Thus, in addition to the return to Mount Gerizim already noted after the forty-seven year exile, a second return is described, apparently in the early Persian period, which led to disputes between the Samaritans, whose civil leader was named Sanballat, and the Jerusalem community under Zerubbabel. It seems more likely that this is a confused use of the biblical material than that there is here evidence of yet another Sanballat. Nor should this reference to Sanballat as the Samaritan civil leader be taken as overthrowing the view set out above[17] that Sanballat was not a Samaritan; the Samaritan material at this period appears to fasten on all opposition to the Jerusalem community as being in itself a good thing, and Sanballat is, as it were, accepted on those grounds, with the story changed to show his success against his Jewish opponents. Comparable confusion is found in the accounts and the order of the Persian rulers. (The Book of Daniel suggests that by the second century B.C. such confusion was already becoming widespread in Jewish tradition.) The tradition that the temple on Mount Gerizim was (re-)built with the permission of Alexander is also found in the Samaritan Chronicle; and here it is difficult to know whether this represents an independent tradition, or whether the Samaritans were dependent upon post-biblical Jewish traditions of the kind represented by Josephus. It is in any case only with the Roman period that an unquestionably independent Samaritan tradition emerges.[18]

From this brief indication of some of the chief features of the Samaritan Chronicle, various conclusions arise. It is doubtful whether much independent light is thrown on the history of the period concerned, though some scholars have argued for a high degree of historical accuracy.[19] The difficulties of such a view have briefly been noted in the outline already given. Perhaps more

[16] Cf. note 4 above.    [17] Above, pp. 58f.
[18] *Encyclopaedia Judaica, Judaica*, art. cit., col. 730.
[19] Cf. note 9 above.

important for our present purpose is the relation between Samaritan and Jewish literary tradition which this Chronicle demonstrates. With regard to the Former Prophets of the Old Testament
canon, this is perhaps not surprising, since Samaritan traditions
with regard to Joshua in particular have long been known. In
addition to this, however, it appears that the reference to Hosea,
Joel and Amos[20] indicates knowledge of the Latter Prophets, and,
much more important, there is the free use made by the Samaritan
work of the Biblical Books of Chronicles. In their final form, these
can scarcely be dated earlier than the fourth century B.C., and it
has, of course, often been alleged that their purpose was anti-
Samaritan. It has already been argued[21] that this is too narrow a
way to look at the purpose of the Chronicler and clearly the Samaritan writers did not so understand it. Rather, we must suppose
that any decisive breach between Jews and Samaritans did not
take place until the Chronicler's work had become generally
accepted within the whole community of Israel. A further point
that emerges in regard to the literary relation between the Old
Testament and the Samaritan material is that Macdonald's
statement, several times repeated, that the Samaritans did not
borrow from the Jews, needs to be modified. It is no doubt true
that there is a sense in which Samaritans and Jews are inheritors
of the same traditions; but in their written form these were clearly
first set down in a Jewish milieu.

Whether any more general conclusions can be reached concerning the early history of Samaritanism from this Chronicle is
doubtful. The implications of the present study as a whole seem
clearly to be that the decisive period for the development of
Samaritanism was that around the turn of the eras. But that is not
to deny that the Samaritans were the heirs of traditions which
went back to a much earlier date—their worship on Mount
Gerizim being the most obvious example. How far such traditions
can be traced within the Samaritan Chronicle is a difficult question.
As the brief summary just given will have indicated, the amount of
material in the Chronicle over and above the biblical sources and
the high-priestly lists is extremely limited, and such material
usually shows traces of historical confusion, to such an extent that
there is really no event recorded of the community in the Chronicle

---

[20] Above, p. 124.          [21] Above, pp. 67–72.

during the Old Testament period of which we can say with real confidence that it is probably historical. As for the high-priestly lists themselves, it is not to be excluded that the names have been correctly preserved, but the dates are extremely suspicious, in so far as the shortest length of a high-priestly reign is nineteen years, and many of them reach much higher numbers.[22] In a succession which allegedly passed from father to son this is frankly incredible.

The importance of the Samaritan Chronicle, therefore, lies much more in the use it makes of Old Testament material, and the theological standpoint it reveals, than in its historical details. Such a judgement could, after all, be passed with regard to the work of the biblical Books of Chronicles, and in neither case should it be intended in a derogatory way. We are already given important indications as to the distinctive standpoint of the Samaritans, and it is these which we must now explore further.

## Samaritan Belief and Practice

The extent of our knowledge of Samaritanism in the last centuries B.C. and at the beginning of the Christian era is severely limited, but enough is known to make a comparison with contemporary Judaism a rewarding exercise. As long ago as 1907 J. A. Montgomery in *The Samaritans* drew together our knowledge of the community in summary form from modern travellers and from such Samaritan literature as was then available. It is worth quoting Montgomery's basic thesis *in extenso*, for the passage of time has only served to corroborate and to illustrate more fully the essential truth of what he then wrote. 'Even as the Samaritans are shown by anthropology to be Hebrews of the Hebrews, so the study of their religion and manners demonstrates them to be nothing else than a Jewish sect.'[23] The themes which he uses to illustrate this basic thesis are still important, and will be referred to frequently in this discussion. It is perhaps worth noting that the more recent study by Macdonald, *The Theology of the*

[22] For details, see Macdonald, op. cit., Appendix IV A, pp. 216f., and M. Gaster, 'The Chain of Samaritan High Priests', in *Studies and Texts*, vol. 1 (New York, 1971 ( =1928) ), pp. 483–502.

[23] Montgomery, op. cit., p. 27.

*Samaritans*, though in many ways more detailed, is less relevant for our present purpose, as the cross-references with Judaism are fewer, and the Samaritan evidence adduced is for the most part from a much later period.[24]

Montgomery's first point is the most fundamental and basic one —the absolute monotheism of the Samaritans. The theme has been brought out more fully by Macdonald, who has shown some of the ways in which Samaritan writers through the ages have explored and explained this belief in the oneness of God, his infinity and omnipotence.[25] No doubt to some extent this was due on the one hand to Islamic influence and on the other to the dangers which they felt to be inherent in the Trinitarianism of the Christians with whom they came into contact, but in any case there is never any suggestion of syncretism, or of any influence from those pagan sources which are alleged to have contributed to the development of Samaritanism. The *shema'* (Deut. 6:4f.) has never attained for Samaritanism the quasi-credal significance that it has for Judaism, but it is an equally definitive element in their sacred scriptures. Montgomery considered that the particular form of this monotheism suggested a link between the Samaritans and the Sadducees, a question to which we shall have to return; here it may simply be noted that increasing knowledge of Judaism makes it possible for this and other characteristic features to be placed in a larger context than was available to Montgomery.

Closely related to this profoundly monotheistic belief is concern for the avoidance of images. Here once again the Jewish roots of this concern are clear enough in the second commandment of the Decalogue (Exod. 20:4–6). Though it may remain a matter for dispute among Old Testament scholars how far the worship of Yahweh was aniconic before the exilic period, it is not in question that in the later Old Testament period there was the most scrupulous avoidance of anything that might be regarded as an image, and here once again Samaritans and Jews were entirely at one. Indeed, such evidence as there is goes to suggest that the Samaritans

---

[24] The warnings of J. Jeremias, *Jerusalem in the Time of Jesus* (London, 1969), p. 352, note 1, that relations between Samaritans and Jews have varied at different periods, in religious as in other aspects, need to be borne in mind; but the basic principles remain unaffected.

[25] Macdonald, op. cit., pp. 65ff.

were even stricter than the Jews in this matter, and regarded the Jerusalem cult with suspicion on these grounds.[26] Of the various allegations brought by Jews against Samaritans, those which imply idolatrous worship in the Temple of Mount Gerizim are among the most ill-founded; these accusations later took the form of a charge that the Samaritans worshipped a dove, and this allegation —completely baseless—was still having to be refuted as late as the nineteenth century.[27] In general terms it would seem that the Samaritans have remained consistent on this whole point, whereas other of the world's religions with which they came into contact— Christianity and Islam as well as Judaism—have known phases of elaborate iconography, often followed by a strong aniconic reaction.

In their conception of God, therefore, and of the manner in which he should be worshipped, Samaritanism and Judaism exhibit a basic similarity. Much the same is true if we consider those areas of religious practice which each group especially stressed. In particular it will be noticed how Samaritanism tends to emphasize the more conservative features of Judaism—just the opposite of what might be expected if Samaritan origins were to be traceable to a syncretistic blend of Judaism and foreign religious practice. A characteristic example is Sabbath-observance: once again, its origins are much disputed; once again, it is clear that in the later Old Testament period the observance of the Sabbath was one of the fundamental characteristics of Judaism. In this respect, once again, Jews and Samaritans were alike. Testimony to Samaritan Sabbath-observance may be found in the Mishnah: 'If a man vowed [to have no benefit] from "them that keep Sabbath", he is forbidden to have benefit from Israelites and from Samaritans' (Tract. Nedarim, 3, 10).[28] (It may be noted in passing that in the same section of this tractate, a distinction is made between Jews and Samaritans on the grounds of places of worship, as we might expect; while on dietary regulations the texts vary, some manuscripts treating Jews and Samaritans alike, others differentiating between them).

Differences in Sabbath-observance did, however, exist between

---

[26] Montgomery, p. 91, note 22.
[27] See Montgomery, Note D, pp. 320f.
[28] In Danby's edition of the Mishnah, p. 267.

the Samaritans and at least some Jews. Judaism developed an elaborate casuistry to determine precisely what might and what might not be done on the Sabbath, and the Mishnah Tractate Shabbath supplies a codified form of this development. The Gospels supply ample evidence of this, and suggest that the niceties of Sabbath-observance were the occasion, at least in some parts of Judaism, of considerable dissatisfaction and dispute. But if the teaching of Jesus and his followers is represented by the saying, 'The Sabbath was made for man, not man for the Sabbath' (MK. 2:27),[29] Samaritanism here would represent the opposite, more conservative, standpoint. Montgomery's description of Samaritan Sabbath-observance is based on modern practice, but it is worth quoting, for in this respect little seems to have changed. 'They stay strictly within doors on the Sabbath, except to go to the synagogue, and have none of the Jewish fiction of the Erub, whereby several houses or a whole street could be artificially designated as a single tenement; nor is there any "Sabbath-day's journey". They follow strictly the injunctions of *Exodus* not to light a fire on the Sabbath, nor may they procure the service of Gentiles for this convenience, as in Judaism; nor may they use any contrivances to keep their food warm, which must all be cooked the day before.'[30] Another instance of the conservatism in this respect of Samaritan practice can be seen in their custom of postponing the slaughter of the Passover lambs if Nisan 14 should fall on a Sabbath.[31] To what extent these Samaritan customs coincided with the practice of other groups within Judaism must for the moment be left open. Certainly, when Samaritan thought about the Sabbath did develop, it did so on lines quite distinct from the casuistry of Judaism, being much more speculative and interested in the idea of the Sabbath as 'an experience, a state'.[32]

Alongside Sabbath-observance may be mentioned the other

---

[29] A closely similar saying is to be found in the Talmud, 'The Sabbath is delivered to you, and you are not delivered to the Sabbath.' For a discussion, see Jeremias, *New Testament Theology*, vol. 1 (London, 1971), p. 18.

[30] Op. cit., p. 33.

[31] W. Förster, *Palestinian Judaism in New Testament Times* (Edinburgh, 1964), p. 174.

[32] Macdonald, op. cit., p. 299. The following section of his work explores the idea further.

distinguishing mark of Judaism—circumcision. Had Samaritanism really been an amalgam of Judaism and practices derived from other religions, one might have expected that the custom of circumcision might have come to be abandoned. This was one of the basic points at issue in the crisis provoked by the attempted hellenization of the Jews, and there are indications that some Jews were ready to abandon the practice (1 Macc. 1:15). We have already noted that it is possible that the Samaritans did not show the same bitter resistance to the policy of Antiochus Epiphanes as did some Jewish groups,[33] but there is no suggestion that this implied a willingness to abandon the practice of circumcision. Instead, all the evidence (admittedly from a later period; but had earlier practice been different, it seems certain that Jewish polemic would have seized upon it) shows that the Samaritans were as strict as the Jews in their insistence on the due performance of the rite. The Masseket Kuthim, one of the additional Tractates appended to the Babylonian Talmud, sets out the custom concerning circumcision: 'An Israelite may circumcise a Samaritan, and a Samaritan an Israelite. R. Juda says: A Samaritan is not to circumcise an Israelite because he circumcises him in nothing else than the name of Mount Gerizim.'[34] The occasion for this contradictory opinion was clearly the fear that the Samaritans might try to win those whom they circumcised away from the worship permitted by Rabbinic Judaism to that of Mount Gerizim, rather than any doubts as to the validity of the rite in itself, or the regularity of its practice. As with Sabbath-observance, the Samaritans show themselves more conservative than the Jews in not allowing the development of any 'traditional' grounds for the postponement of circumcision, its performance upon the eighth day being very strictly insisted upon.[35] There are, indeed, occasional instances in Samaritan history of literary attacks against the Jews as being 'the uncircumcised', not apparently because of any irregularity in practice, but because in Samaritan eyes they had forfeited any claim to be the true Israel.[36] This rigour of observance gave rise

[33] Above, p. 88.
[34] Quoted by Montgomery, p. 199. The whole of Masseket Kuthim is there set out.
[35] Montgomery, p. 42.
[36] Macdonald, op. cit., pp. 294f.

to the widely quoted dictum of Rabbi Simon ben Gamaliel: 'Every command the Samaritans keep, they are more scrupulous in observing than Israel.'[37]

Other parallels might be added to this list as showing links between Samaritan practice and that of later Judaism, but for the most part they would add little to the argument, being either chronologically uncertain, or of a very general nature, as in the similar ethical emphases which developed in Samaritanism and Judaism. There are, however, two further points which may be cited as showing links between Jews and Samaritans which had not involved any decisive breach before the very latest Old Testament period. The first concerns the synagogue, the second the festal calendar.

We have already noted that the origin of Sabbath-observance and of circumcision is obscure. The same is true with the beginnings of the synagogue. It is commonly held that it originated among the exiles in Babylon, but this is no more than conjecture based upon what is held to have been inherently probable among a community driven away from the Temple.[38] Whether or not this view is accepted, the earliest evidence for their existence certainly comes from the Judaism of the diaspora, from the third century B.C. onwards;[39] there is no reference to synagogues in Palestine before the Christian era. (Ps. 74:8, which speaks of 'synagogues of God' in the AV and RV translations, should not be understood so precisely, as the more modern translations make clear, nor can such a reference be found by suggesting a Maccabaean date for the Psalm, as was once quite widely held.) It appears, therefore, that the New Testament affords us our earliest indisputable evidence for the existence of synagogues in Palestine, though by that time they were clearly well established, so that they must have been in existence before the Christian era.

As for the Samaritan synagogue, our knowledge of its development is even more limited, but once again it is clear that there were Samaritan synagogues both in Palestine and among the

---

[37] Montgomery, p. 170.

[38] See Rowley, *Worship in Ancient Israel* (London, 1967), Ch. 7, (esp. pp. 224ff.) for this view; Ackroyd, *Exile and Restoration*, pp. 32ff., prefers to leave the question open.

[39] Reicke, op. cit., pp. 119ff.

diaspora early in the Christian era.[40] In general it is apparent that in Samaritanism as in Judaism the synagogue played an important part, undergoing a similar development even down to minor details,[41] and such development can scarcely have begun earlier than the last pre-Christian centuries. The common roots of the two faiths in the period around the turn of the eras is again illustrated.

The other feature common to Judaism and Samaritanism which demands some notice is the calendar, and in particular the feasts. In modern times a great many visitors to Palestine from Europe and elsewhere have been able to observe, and to participate at least as spectators in, the Samaritan Passover, and in this as in the other chief festivals the requirements of the Pentateuch (Lev. 23) are carried out. The many vicissitudes of their history—times of persecution, expulsion from Mount Gerizim, calendrical disputes —all have contributed to numerous differences in detail from Jewish observance, but both are clearly rooted, as we should expect, in the provisions of the Old Testament.

What would be much more remarkable, if it could be substantiated, is a reference to the keeping of the feast of Purim. This oblique way of expressing the matter is necessary, for there appears to be no recent statement of the observance of this feast, the last reference to it being J. Mills' *Three Months Residence at Nablus, and an Account of the Modern Samaritans* published in 1864. Mills' account is circumstantial, setting out details of the keeping of the feast, and the way it differs from Jewish observance, together with Samaritan speculation about the force of the name, Purim.[42] If such a custom has indeed been observed among the Samaritans from antiquity, it would be a further very strong pointer to the late date of the final separation between Samaritans and Jews. While there is no general agreement on the antiquity of

[40] The evidence concerning Samaritan synagogues is drawn together by Kippenberg, op. cit., pp. 145–71.

[41] Montgomery, op. cit., pp. 28ff.

[42] Mills, op. cit., pp. 266f. The Samaritan observance is stated there to take place in the month Shabat, not Adar; is given a Pentateuchal association by being linked with Moses' mission to deliver Israel from Egypt rather than with Esther; and is said to mean 'Rejoicings' rather than 'Lots'. These differences could represent Samaritan modifications, or they may imply a totally different origin for this Samaritan festival.

Purim, or of the book of Esther in which it is described, it is usually held that the feast was probably not introduced into Palestine before the second century B.C., though it may have been observed earlier in the diaspora. The earliest reference to Purim outside the book of Esther is at 2 Maccabees 15:36. We have already commented[43] on the difficulty of dating this work, but in any case it can be no earlier than the late second century B.C., and a late date for Esther has been argued by some scholars on the grounds that it is the only Old Testament book unrepresented among the Qumran scrolls. In short, this late arrival in Palestinian Judaism provides another indication of continuing links between Samaritans and Jews in the latest pre-Christian period.

In all the points that have thus far been made, the basic features of Samaritan belief and practice have been seen to be very closely akin to those of Judaism, the differences being only of a kind which mark out the Samaritans as more conservative than Rabbinic Judaism came to be. One might well feel tempted to ask why Samaritans and Jews ever parted, and what distinguished them from each other. It is to these differences that we must now give attention.

## Judaeo-Samaritan Disputes

Among different Christian groups it is often the case that those which to the outsider might seem indistinguishable in faith and practice can be those whose disputes with one another are the most bitter. Such seems to have been the state of affairs between Jews and Samaritans at the beginning of the Christian era. The point is well brought out by J. Jeremias, who begins his treatment thus: 'Descending to the lowest degree of the scale (sc: of racial purity), we come to the Samaritans.'[44] He goes on to show that, though the Samaritans were sometimes and in some circumstances classed with Gentiles, at other times a difference was clearly made. There are references to Samaritans being allowed into the inner court of the Jerusalem Temple,[45] and a number of New

---

[43] Above, pp. 87f.
[44] Jeremias, *Jerusalem in the Time of Jesus*, p. 352.
[45] Ibid., p. 353.

Testament passages suggest that it was possible to travel from Galilee to Judah by way of the Samaritan area. It was recognized, too, that the Samaritans claimed patriarchal descent (John 4:12), and that they were scrupulous observers of the Torah.

In the light of all this it becomes appropriate to look again at the New Testament passage with which this study began. At the outset the traditional translation, 'Jews have no dealings with Samaritans', was accepted as at least giving an indication of a widespread state of affairs, but it was noted then that this phrase creates more problems than might at first sight appear. Its textual history has led to a division of opinion among commentators whether it should be regarded as part of the original text of the gospel,[46] and it is in any case to be taken as a comment by the evangelist rather than as a part of the Samaritan woman's speech. More important, however, is the doubt concerning the correct translation. The verb in the passage, συνχρασθαι, is not found elsewhere with the general sense of 'have dealings with', but rather seems to mean 'use together'. This might suggest a more precise meaning for this passage. The Tractate Niddah of the Mishnah states: 'The daughters of the Samaritans are [deemed unclean as] menstruants from their cradle.'[47] This was regarded as ground for refusal to use vessels in common with the Samaritans, and it may be that the evangelist's note here has reference to the same point. The New English Bible has followed this view and translates, 'Jews and Samaritans, it should be noted, do not use vessels in common'.[48]

The Mishnah and the fourth Gospel, then, may give evidence of hostility in the first century A.D. between Jews and Samaritans, but the underlying cause of such hostility is still not indicated. We may obtain further clues concerning the basis of this hostility by looking again at Masseket Kuthim, the late date of which makes

---

[46] In addition to the various commentaries, see the note by J. N. Birdsall in *The Cambridge History of the Bible*, Vol. 1, edited by P. R. Ackroyd and C. F. Evans (Cambridge, 1970), p. 375; the omission of the phrase in two major codices leads him to the conclusion that it is an interpretative gloss.

[47] Niddah 4.1. Danby's edition, p. 748.

[48] On the interpretation of this passage, see D. Daube, 'Jesus and the Samaritan Woman: the Meaning of συνχρασθαι', *JBL*, 69, 1950, pp. 137ff.

its uncritical use dangerous, but which does provide a significant comment on Judaeo-Samaritan relations. In its last halakah is the question: 'When shall we take them back?', to which the answer is: 'When they renounce Mount Gerizim and confess Jerusalem and the resurrection of the dead. From this time forth he that robs a Samaritan shall be as he who robs an Israelite.'[49]

The two areas of difference here set out are obviously highly significant—not least for what they omit. There is, for example, no requirement that the Samaritans should first accept more than the Torah as sacred scripture. The phrase used, 'take them back', is also striking, since it seems to look upon the Samaritans as basically a group that had broken away from the Jews rather than as one which was essentially foreign in its roots. But the real heart of the dispute is centred upon the issue of rival holy places and different eschatological beliefs. A third point which will have to be taken into account, that of true priesthood, may for the moment be regarded as one aspect of the dispute concerning the holy places. We must consider these matters of dispute somewhat more fully.

It has already been noted on more than one occasion that one of the characteristic themes of the Chronicler was the great stress on Jerusalem as the only place proper to the worship of Yahweh, and the building of the Samaritan Temple on Mount Gerizim would clearly add more point to such an emphasis. We tend to assume that this attitude to Jerusalem as *the* holy place was universal within Judaism, but there is in fact a good deal of evidence which suggests a much more ambivalent attitude among some groups. In so far as earliest Christianity was itself a Jewish sect, the New Testament provides some evidence along these lines, though its precise interpretation is clearly a matter for dispute, particularly in view of the destruction of Jerusalem in A.D. 70 before most of the New Testament writings had reached their final form. Thus, Jesus' laments over Jerusalem are often regarded as *vaticinia ex eventu* by the evangelists (cf. especially Luke 19:41 ff.). On the other hand, some scholars, notably M. Simon, have seen in Stephen's speech in Acts, with its strong repudiation of the Temple (7:48ff.). an echo of a line of thought rejecting the Jerusalem Temple and traceable within the Old Testament and

[49] Quoted in Montgomery, op. cit., p. 203.

at Qumran.[50] The idea has indeed been put forward that Stephen's very positive attitude to the Pentateuch and the Tabernacle and his disparaging description of Israel's later history might suggest that he was himself a Samaritan, and it has been argued that the pentateuchal quotations in his speech reflect the Samaritan version.[51] Rather than so precise an identification, however, it may be better to see in Stephen's speech and in Samaritanism variant forms of the same attitude of rejection of the claims of Jerusalem.

But this negative attitude to Jerusalem and its cultus is found in other areas of Judaism also. Some indication of this had long been known from Josephus' description of the factionalism that was clearly an extremely potent force among the Jews until the very last days of their struggle against the Romans, but the evidence in the *Jewish War* is scanty and cannot be corroborated from other sources. More recently, the scrolls from Qumran have provided clearer evidence from another quarter. There, the Jerusalem priesthood are those 'who shall amass money and wealth by plundering the peoples',[52] and 'there shall be no more joining the house of Judah'.[53] Some scholars have alleged that the entire Jerusalem cultus was repudiated by the Qumran covenanters; it may be that the evidence is too slender for so definite a conclusion, but we can at least see that there was a marked hostility to some of the claims made on behalf of the Jerusalem temple.[54]

Here again, therefore, the Samaritans fit logically into the context of the Judaism of the beginning of the Christian era. They

[50] M. Simon, *St. Stephen and the Hellenists* (London, 1958). O. Cullmann has also argued that opposition to the worship of the Jerusalem Temple is an element common to the Qumran community, the Fourth Gospel, and the Hellenists in Acts. ('The Significance of the Qumran Texts for Research into the Beginnings of Christianity', in *The Scrolls and the New Testament*, edited by K. Stendahl (London, 1958), pp. 18–32.)

[51] W. F. Albright and C. S. Mann, 'Stephen's Samaritan Background', in J. Munck, *The Acts of the Apostles*, AB (New York, 1967), pp. 285ff.

[52] 'Habakkuk Commentary IX' (Vermes, *The Dead Sea Scrolls in English* (Harmondsworth, 1962), p. 238).

[53] 'Damascus Rule IV' (Vermes, p. 101).

[54] See S. E. Johnson, 'The Dead Sea Manual of Discipline and the Jerusalem Church of Acts', in Stendahl, *The Scrolls and the New Testament*, p. 136, for the view of complete rejection; Rowley, 'The Qumran Sect and Christian Origins', in *From Moses to Qumran*, p. 247 and note 2, is more cautious.

shared with other groups a hostile attitude towards Jerusalem, but differed from them by insisting that Gerizim was the holy mountain upon which God was to be worshipped. It is also relevant here to bear in mind that the Pharisaic groups which evolved into the dominant type of Rabbinic Judaism showed no decrease in veneration for Jerusalem after its fall. A Jerusalem-mystique continued and developed within Judaism, and any rejection of Jerusalem was regarded as being in itself treacherous. In one sense the controversies between Judaism and the Christian church may be taken as illustrative of this; certainly it was a point of issue between Jews and Samaritans.

Before turning to the other requirement of Masseket Kuthim it is instructive at this point to consider the question related to that of the right holy place—that of the right priesthood. If the rival claims of Jerusalem and Gerizim provided a continuing background for controversy, the way in which that controversy was carried on from one generation to another was through rival claims concerning priesthood.

We may note at the outset that it is clear from other sources that the exercise of the Jerusalem priesthood, and in particular of the high-priestly office, in the second century B.C. was a matter which occasioned much bitterness. The description in 2 Maccabees 4 of the succession of high-priests at the time of Antiochus Epiphanes is a clear, though no doubt one-sided, illustration of this, and disputes over the high-priestly office continued down into the Roman period. It is easy to see that occasion may well have been given for those hostile to the claims of Jerusalem—be they Qumran covenanters or Samaritans—to feel that their suspicions were justified. It is in such a context that the variant traditions already noted concerning true priesthood at the time of Eli should be understood;[55] it was considered of great importance to establish a claim to a truly legitimate priesthood. In this light, too, Josephus' story of the establishment of the Samaritan Temple takes on a new significance. We have seen already that it must be regarded with considerable reserve from the historical point of view, but it may well provide further pointers towards a division between Jews and Samaritans concerning priesthood. If the story of Manasses in *Antiquities* XI has any historical basis, it is most likely to be in

[55] Above, pp. 120f.

rivalries within the Jerusalem priesthood which were resolved by one group leaving Jerusalem and establishing itself in the ancient site of Shechem. Whether this was in fact the origin of the Samaritan community must remain an open question; it certainly illustrates the kind of difference that existed between Jews and Samaritans.[56]

An attempt to give greater precision to this divergence concerning priesthood has been made by J. Bowman.[57] His starting-point is the fact that it became important, from the sixth century B.C. onwards, to claim Zadokite descent to establish true priesthood. This theme is first found in Ezekiel 40–8, where several passages insist on a distinction between the Zadokites and the remaining Levites; it is an integral element in the priestly genealogy of 1 Chronicles 6:3–15; the Qumran Scrolls regularly speak of the priests as 'sons of Zadok'; and the Samaritans also lay claim to Zadokite priesthood. On this basis Bowman suggests that this Zadokite claim may be traceable to the disputes to which we have just referred, and that the grandson of Eliashib, expelled by Nehemiah (Neh. 13:28), perhaps to be identified with Josephus' 'Manasses', may be the connecting link. On this view the Samaritans would have been able to claim a true descent for their own priesthood; they would be able to point to the impurity of the Jerusalem priesthood in view of the subsequent struggles for supremacy there; and they could cite in their favour Ezekiel 37:15ff., with its picture of the joining of Ephraim and Judah without any suggestion of the impurity of Ephraim.

Such an attempt to tie up a number of loose ends in interesting and ingenious, but it is doubtful whether it can be sustained. The reconstruction appears to suffer from two serious weaknesses. In the first place, the Zadokite links of the Samaritans are extremely tenuous. There is a Zadok in the line of Samaritan high-priests, but he cannot be identified with the Zadok of the time of David, and the references cited by Bowman from the Samaritan Chronicle III (the Tolidah) are extremely confused chronologically. There are references to Zadok in Chronicle II, and these are relatively

---

[56] The possible relevance of this Josephus story for Samaritan origins has been worked out by Kippenberg, op. cit., pp. 50–9.

[57] J. Bowman, 'Ezekiel and the Zadokite Priesthood', *TGUOS*, 16, 1955–6, pp. 1–14.

favourable, particularly in the story of the succession to David (Sam. Chr. II: I Kings I); but this does not seem to be anything more than a deliberate contrast with his contemporary Abiathar, whose descent from Eli was enough to discredit him in Samaritan eyes. The second objection to Bowman's theory is that it attempts to be much too precise in reconstructing the history behind the story in Nehemiah and that in Josephus. Rowley has pointed out how many questions are begged at this point, and concludes that there is no real evidence for a Zadokite claim on the part of the Samaritans.[58] It seems, therefore, that the precise cause of the division concerning priesthood must remain obscure, though the quarrels of the second century B.C. do much to illustrate it.

Returning now to the requirements of Masseket Kuthim, the other point at issue concerned eschatological beliefs, and, more specifically, an acknowledgement of the resurrection. It is generally maintained that belief in a blessed future life was a late development in Judaism, with the first certain attestation being Daniel 12:2, about 165 B.C. From that period until the final triumph of what may in general be termed a Pharisaic type of Judaism, this question of an after-life was one of the most fiercely debated issues within Judiasm.[59] The point is amply illustrated in the New Testament by such episodes as Jesus' dispute with the Sadducees (Mark 12:18–27//), or Paul before the Sanhedrin dividing his accusers by introducing the question of resurrection (Acts 23:6–9). It appears that in its earlier stages Samaritanism would have sided with the Sadducees on this matter in rejecting the idea of resurrection. Here once again the Samaritans appear as a conservative element within Judaism. Certainly, this reserve with regard to resurrection is a strong pointer against any suggestion of syncretism or pagan origins, for in such circumstances belief in some form of future life seems to have been almost universal.

Among the Samaritans, however, as with the Jews, disputes arose on the question of a future life, and this appears to have been

---

[58] Rowley, *Sanballat and the Samaritan Temple*, pp. 264f.; cf. also the criticisms made by Kippenberg, op. cit., pp. 65f.

[59] The variety of views within Judaism and the even greater variety of modern assessments of them, is illustrated by C. F. Evans, *Resurrection and the New Testament* (London, 1970), esp. pp. 19f.

a central issue in the division between the main body of Samaritans and various sects which arose. In regard to the best-known of the sects, the Dositheans, the evidence is extremely puzzling. Both Montgomery and T. Caldwell have felt that the only possible interpretation is to suppose that there were two separate sects named after men called Dositheus (a very common Samaritan name), one denying the resurrection, the other a later group of an enthusiastic type which proclaimed the resurrection and beliefs of a millenarian kind.[60] The inherent implausibility of such a view, however, has led others to find an explanation of the apparent contradiction. Both Bowman and Kippenberg have regarded the apparently irreconcilable views attributed to the Dositheans as due to falsification or misunderstanding on the part of their opponents, who were prepared to lay any charge against them regardless of consistency or logic.[61] However this may be, it appears that it was only in the fourth century A.D., in the time of Marqah, that a formulated and generally accepted doctrine of a blessed future life emerged within Samaritanism, the innate conservatism of the community being once again illustrated.[62]

Before leaving this area of doctrine, we may briefly consider more general aspects of eschatology, of which this is an important part. Certain themes again emerge which place Samaritanism within the context of the Judaism of the last pre-Christian centuries. At a later date Samaritanism was much occupied with the idea of the day of vengeance and of recompense, a time when the sufferings of the community would be justified; but other aspects of Samaritan eschatology show particular associations with Jewish ideas of the end of the Old Testament period. Two points are especially noteworthy: messianic expectations, and the belief that the world's history could be divided into clearly defined periods.

It is generally agreed that a characteristic feature of the Judaism

[60] Montgomery, op. cit., pp. 261ff.; Caldwell, 'Dositheos Samaritanus', *Kairos* IV, 2, 1962, pp, 105–17.

[61] Bowman, *Samaritanische Probleme* (Stuttgart, 1967), p. 37; Kippenberg, op. cit., pp. 135ff.

[62] See Macdonald, *Theology*, pp. 372ff., for a full discussion of the belief in its later forms in Samaritanism.

of the later Old Testament period was the development of a variety of forms of messianic expectation, without any one form of that expectation becoming the norm.[63] Among the Samaritans this messianism was expressed under the figure of the 'taheb', a word which appears to be derived from the Aramaic form of the Hebrew *šūb*, to return. In the participial form which is used, the meaning may be 'the one who restores' or 'the one who returns'.[64] Each could claim support from Samaritan exegesis of texts in Deuteronomy: the former from Deuteronomy 18:18, with its expectation of the Lord raising up a prophet like Moses; the latter from Deuteronomy 32, pictured as presaging the return of Moses as the prologue to the expected time of divine favour. In either case there is a clear parallel in thought here to the Jewish expectation of a Davidic Messiah, and an even closer link with the expectation of a Messiah of the house of Joseph which appears to have been current in some circles. Mowinckel has suggested the possibility that 'the thought of the Messiah ben Joseph . . . arose among the Samaritans as a counterpart of the Jewish messiah of the house of David, but that it was occasionally accepted in Jewish circles'.[65] Certainly the late Old Testament period was a formative age for the development of such beliefs, which are characteristic of both Judaism and Samaritanism.

Linked with this messianic expectation, especially in the exegesis of Deuteronomy 32, is the idea of the 'day of vengeance' (cf. especially v. 35). Although the idea of a 'day of Yahweh' is at least as early as the eighth-century prophets (Amos 5:18), by the time of the apocalyptic writings it had taken on a very different form. In Daniel and other apocalyptic works the theme is found that the present time of troubles should be regarded as a final time of testing before God brought deliverance to his faithful people and punishment of their enemies. It was the theme of punishment which occupied most attention, and is prominent in Samaritan as well as

[63] See the very full discussion in S. Mowinckel, *He that cometh* (Oxford, 1956), Part II, pp. 261ff.

[64] Montgomery, p. 246. For a full discussion, see now Kippenberg, op. cit., pp. 276–305.

[65] Mowinckel, op. cit., p. 290. A contrary view is expressed by Bowman, 'Early Samaritan Eschatology', *JJS*, 6, 1956, pp. 63–72; cf. also Kippenberg, op cit., pp. 265ff.

in Jewish and Christian writings of this period. In particular, the phrase 'day of vengeance' is found in the Samaritan (and also the LXX) form of Deuteronomy 32:35, and while such an idea is too widespread for it to be possible to claim its origin in one specific milieu, we may certainly note that here once again we have an idea common to Samaritanism and the Judaism of the last pre-Christian centuries, harassed as it was by the threat of superior worldly powers.

Rather more specific is the accompanying notion that history is divisible into a number of clearly defined ages. Whether the idea is native to Judaism or is derived from Zoroastrian thought, it is clearly expressed in Daniel 2 and 7, with their picture of the world successively dominated by four great empires. In the pseudepigraphical books there are many variations on this theme, which is not characteristic of the earlier Old Testament. In Samaritanism it takes the form of belief in ages of disfavour (*panuta*) and of favour (*ridwan* or *rahuta*). The first age of disfavour had been from the time of Adam's sin to the time of Noah; the second, as already noted in our consideration of the Samaritan Chronicle II, had begun at the schism of Eli and would continue until the hoped-for arrival of the taheb. The first great time of favour had been from Noah to Samson, and the second would be inaugurated by the taheb. It has been suggested that there are links with themes expressed in the Qumran literature,[66] but however this may be, we find here a type of thought especially characteristic of late Judaism.

Even more than in other sections of this study, this consideration of Samaritan beliefs has had to be of a cursory and superficial nature. To give a more extended treatment would greatly extend the range of what is here being undertaken, and, fortunately, the recent works of Macdonald and Kippenberg go far to provide the materials for such fuller consideration. Nevertheless, even such an outline picture shows how close were the links—even in disagreement—between Samaritanism and the Judaism of the turn of the eras. Much could no doubt be explained in other ways, and certainly many characteristic aspects of Samaritanism only

[66] Macdonald, *Theology*, p. 261. He cites no specific passage, and I am unable to find anything in the published Qumran material that is as explicit as the Samaritan form of this belief.

developed at a later period still. Nevertheless, there appear to be no characteristic practices or doctrines which could best be explained as resulting from a split from the main body of Judaism earlier than the second, or possibly the third, century B.C. Still less is there any sign of the syncretistic origin which anti-Samaritan polemic has so often suggested as the community's real background.

## The Samaritan Pentateuch

Almost no mention has so far been made of the Samaritan Pentateuch. It has, however, commonly been regarded as having important light to throw on the origins of Samaritanism, and it is therefore necessary to consider the evidence that it affords. Its bearing is twofold—the evidence of the text itself, and its importance for ideas of canonicity. It may first of all be useful to outline briefly the way in which the Samaritan Pentateuch has often been used in the attempt to establish the date of a Samaritan schism, and it should then be possible to set out more clearly the difficulties in such a view.

The kind of argument which has commonly been set out runs along these lines. The Samaritans accept as sacred scripture the Torah, but not the other two divisions of the Hebrew Old Testament, the Prophets and the Writings. The implication of this would seem to be that the Samaritans separated from the Jews at a date when the Torah was already held to be sacrosanct, but the other sections were not yet treated with the same veneration. The general critical view of the dates of composition of various parts of the Old Testament has suggested that the Pentateuch was substantially complete by about the fifth century, and this corresponded well with the Jewish tradition associating Ezra with the promulgation of the Torah. Any date from the time of Ezra would then be possible for the Samaritan schism, but too late a date would, on this view, be ruled out by the Samaritans' non-acceptance of the Prophets and the Writings. No firm consensus of critical opinion has been reached for the dating of the latest additions to the prophetic collection, but references in Ecclesiasticus from the early second century B.C.—particularly 49:10, which speaks of 'the twelve prophets'—suggest that a prophetic corpus was by then well established, so that allusion could be made to it without the likelihood of misunderstanding. This would suggest a date no later than the third century for its canonization, and would imply that the Samaritan schism had already taken place by that period. The dates of the Septuagint translation have sometimes been adduced as additional support for this position, but evidence concerning the origins of the LXX is so scanty and unreliable that no great weight could be placed upon it. All in all, however, it appeared as if a strong case could be made for a Samaritan schism which must have occurred in the fourth century or the early part of the third, after the canonization of the Torah, but before that of the Prophets or the Writings.

This reconstruction, attractive though it appears, is nevertheless open to objection on two main grounds. The first is external to it, and concerns the textual characteristics of the Samaritan Pentateuch, which the argument set out above did not need to take into account. The second is inherent in that argument, in that it envisages a process of canonization much less complex than the available history suggests. We shall need to consider each of these objections in turn. It might be possible to speak of a third objection, in so far as some of the critical presuppositions set out above have come under attack, but that lies outside the present area of discussion.

If the text of the Samaritan Pentateuch was referred to in the type of argument already outlined, it was usually thought to lend support to it, since the Samaritan version preserves the old Hebrew script, whereas in Judaism the use of the square or Aramaic script (Mishnah: 'Assyrian script') became general. Prima facie, therefore, this suggested the divergence of the Samaritan script from the main Jewish tradition before the use of the square script became general. It has, however, long been recognized that the palaeography of the Samaritan version could not be so simply explained. W. F. Albright, for example, drew attention to the similarities between the Samaritan script and the Hasmonaean coins of the late second and early first centuries,[67] and more recently examination of old Hebrew fragments from Qumran,

[67] W. F. Albright, *From the Stone Age to Christianity* (2nd edn.; New York, 1957), pp. 345f.

together with a wider range of coins now available, has strengthened that conclusion. It seems that there was a survival—and indeed a development in form—of the old Hebrew script right down into the Christian era. J. D. Purvis has recently published a very full examination of the textual problems of the Samaritan Pentateuch, and, though some of his arguments have been criticized in detail, as we shall see, here his conclusions seem incontrovertible. 'The direct parentage of the Samaritan script was the palaeo-Hebrew of the Hasmonaean period. . . . The Samaritan script represents a departure from the palaeo-Hebrew at the stage of development which the script had reached at that time. By no stretch of the imagination can the Samaritan script be considered a script that had broken off from the palaeo-Hebrew at an earlier time to experience a similar, concurrent development.'[68]

From the script itself Purvis turns to the consideration of orthography. (For the non-Hebraist, it may be helpful to explain that the letters of the Hebrew alphabet are all basically consonants, but that some of them may be used as vowels (cf. the English letter 'y'). Custom has varied greatly as to the extent to which these letters should be inserted in the written text as an aid to the reader, and it is this custom which is here under consideration.) Conclusions are here inevitably somewhat more tentative. In the matter of the actual formation of letters a clear basis for comparison is available in the coins and manuscript fragments that have survived; in the matter of orthography, on the other hand, it is much more difficult to establish a satisfactory basis for comparison. No single orthographically acceptable form of the Samaritan Pentateuch has yet been established, and all the available published texts have been the subject of criticism.[69] (The same difficulty is inherent in the criticism of the Massoretic text, but the Samaritan has received a much smaller measure of critical study.)

With these limitations in mind, Purvis argues that there is at least the probability that the orthography of the Samaritan

---

[68] Purvis, *The Samaritan Pentateuch and the Origin of the Samaritan Sect*, pp. 50f.

[69] Purvis has recognized the difficulty here, but has still been criticized as being willing to rely on an inadequate basis of evidence. See the reviews of his work by Macdonald in *JJS*, XXI, 1970, pp. 69ff., and by B. J. Roberts in *JTS*, NS, XX, 1969, pp. 569ff.

Pentateuch, like its palaeography, is that of the Hasmonaean period. The Samaritan text tends towards a fuller orthography, by the use of *matres lectionis* (vowel-letters) where they are not found in the Massoretic text, and such evidence as is available again suggests that this tendency was characteristic of the Hasmonaean period. Purvis emphatically rejects the suggestion that the Samaritan orthography is a medieval development.

It is scarcely possible to do more than note the main conclusions of recent examination of Samaritan palaeography and orthography in a study of this kind, the main concerns of which are historical. The third area with which Purvis deals may, however, be considered somewhat more fully. This is the textual tradition in which the Samaritan Pentateuch stands. It has already been mentioned[70] that for a long period after the rediscovery of the Samaritan Pentateuch by the western world in the early seventeenth century, its textual evidence was used in controversies between Protestants and Roman Catholics, the former disparaging it as of secondary significance, the latter upholding in on the (very misleading) ground that it supported the LXX against the Massoretic Text. In more recent times many theories have been put forward with regard to the history of the transmission of the text of the Old Testament, and—though no longer motivated by sectarian considerations—controversy remains as bitter as ever.

Within the very wide range of views put forward, two may be noted which bear more directly upon the Samaritan Pentateuch. A. Sperber has argued that the Samaritan text represents a Northern Israelite local tradition, just as the Massoretic text represents a corresponding Southern tradition. Were it to be generally upheld, this theory would lend support to those views which see in Samaritanism a long-standing distinction from the Judaism of Jerusalem. In fact, however, Sperber's views have not for the most part won acceptance. As S. Talmon has noted, they depend upon a transference into the textual realm of geographical divisions, comparable to the sigla J and E of Pentateuchal criticism, for which there is no inherent support.[71]

The other theory of textual transmission is of more immediate relevance, for it is that which Purvis himself follows. It is associated

[70] Above, p. 6.
[71] S. Talmon, in *The Cambridge History of the Bible*, Vol. 1, p. 181.

especially with the name of F. M. Cross,[72] who, on the basis of his studies of the text-forms of the Qumran material, has arrived at a theory of three text-types or families, which he has called 'Palestinian', 'Egyptian' and (with some hesitation) 'Babylonian'. Cross himself has noted the significance of the Samaritan text in this analysis, and this has been carried a stage further by Purvis, who categorizes the Samaritan as 'a Palestinian text type descended from an old Palestinian textual tradition'.[73] He further argues that the Samaritan text has been influenced by the 'Babylonian' type, which was only introduced into Palestine in the first century B.C., and concludes that the Samaritan Pentateuch cannot have undergone its final redaction earlier than the first century B.C., and may have been influenced by Jewish tradition at an even later date.

This whole theory of local texts has yet to make its way as a satisfactory explanation of the complicated phenomena that demand consideration. This is partly because Cross has not yet published the major study of the subject which he has announced, partly because some caution seems to be needed in view of the vagaries in the preservation of ancient texts. One textual tradition has been preserved in the Christian church, which is largely that of the LXX; two others have survived in the synagogue—the Massoretic and the Samaritan; fragments of another have become known to us because of the climate and inaccessibility of the Qumran area. There may well have been other local variations of textual transmission, evidence for which has disappeared completely. The 'local text' theory, therefore, remains no more than an attractive hypothesis, and in order not to lay too much weight upon it, we should say only that the indications of the textual history of the Samaritan Pentateuch may give further indications that the Hasmonaean age, and no earlier period, was the decisive epoch of the distinctive Samaritan recension.[74]

The other relevant aspect of the theory outlined at the beginning of this section is the question of canonicity. Here two related

[72] It has not been fully worked out in a major study, but Cross has devoted a series of articles in journals to his views. See especially 'The Contribution of the Qumran Discoveries to the Study of the Hebrew Text', *IEJ*, 16, 1966, pp. 81–95.

[73] Op. cit., p. 80.

[74] For a criticism of the 'local text' theory, see Talmon in *The Cambridge History of the Bible*, vol. 1, pp. 193–8.

questions are involved. First, from the Samaritan side: what is implied by the 'acceptance' of the Pentateuch and 'rejection' of other books of the Old Testament? Secondly, in terms of the more general notion of canonical scripture, what is known of different attitudes to the canon among Jewish groups at about the beginning of the Christian era?

Some indication has already been given[75] that to speak of 'rejection' as the Samaritan attitude to the Prophets and the Writings is misleading. It is clear that the process of canonization of these books was a slow and gradual one, and there must clearly have been a time when they were widely known and accorded great respect, without being regarded as holy scripture. We have had numerous occasions to note the conservatism of the Samaritans, and here we find another example of it. They clung to an attitude which in many other Jewish circles was passing away, of treating some at least of these books with respect, but not as sacred scripture. The evidence for such an attitude varies, as would be expected, between the different biblical books, in some cases being considerable, in others nonexistent—there are some biblical books of which Samaritan tradition reveals no knowledge. (The same could be said of the New Testament's use of the Old.) The most extensive use of non-Pentateuchal material is concentrated, as we have seen, on the Former Prophets, with Joshua in particular being a subject of great interest in Samaritanism. The history and traditions underlying these books were held to belong as much to the Samaritans as to the people of Judah. The same could be said of the work of the Chronicler. In other cases something much closer to 'rejection' can properly be spoken of, particularly in cases where a work was very obviously Jerusalem-centred, or where a prophet was pictured as speaking in the name of Yahweh. The Samaritans, as we have seen, accept no prophet but Moses, and so they reject all other writings that claim to be prophetic—that is to say, our 'Latter Prophets'. (Whether this is linked with the rejection of the prophetic office shown in such passages as Zechariah 13:2–6 must remain an open question.)

If we pass to our second question, concerning different attitudes to the canon among Jewish groups at the turn of the eras, some interesting points emerge. It is commonly held, on the basis of

[75] Above, pp. 110f.

Josephus, *Antiquities*, XIII, 297, that the Sadducees also regarded only the Pentateuch as canonical. Links between the Sadducees and the Samaritans have already been noted in the matter of eschatology, and the question of the relation between the two groups will arise again later; but for the moment we should certainly note that such a correspondence in belief concerning the extent of the canon at once invalidates the argument that Samaritan non-acceptance of the Prophets and the Writings automatically implies a break from the mainstream of Judaism in the fourth or third century

It has often been held that the Jews of Alexandria had a more extensive canon than those of Palestine, on the basis of those works found in the LXX which have not found a place in the Hebrew Bible. It has been persuasively argued by G. W. Anderson that the true situation was, in fact, precisely the opposite, and that there too it was the Torah which was regarded as the truly sacred collection, with other books being given only a secondary place. The bases for this conclusion are the extreme accuracy of the LXX rendering of the Pentateuch compared with its freedom elsewhere; the reference to the Pentateuch in the Letter of Aristeas, from which most of our fragmentary knowledge about LXX origins is gained; and the great stress laid on the Torah by Philo.[76] In other words, the 'wider canon' of Alexandria is really a product of the Christian church.

The other group to which it is natural to look for evidence of a canon differing from that which became normal is the Qumran covenanters. The evidence is not entirely clear, though the quantity of scriptural material among the Qumran scrolls makes it apparent that a canon approximating to the normal Palestinian one was accepted. Doubts arise as to Esther, of which—uniquely among Old Testament books—no fragments have been found at Qumran, as has already been noted,[77] and as to the Psalms, since Old Testament and other Psalms have been found juxtaposed in Qumran manuscripts. In this latter case, however, it is probable that these were anthologies, whose precise purpose is unknown, but which do not derogate from the canonicity of the biblical Psalter.

[76] G. W. Anderson, 'Canonical and Non-Canonical', in *The Cambridge History of the Bible*, vol. 1, pp. 145–9.
[77] Above, p. 138.

If we attempt now to summarize the argument from the Samaritan Pentateuch in so far as it bears on our knowledge of the origins of the community, it appears that the textual evidence—and the palaeography in particular—suggests a recension in the Hasmonaean age. In this respect it is noteworthy that, just as many Jewish charges against the Samaritans seem to lack a factual basis, so here the Samaritans' charge against Ezra concerning the changing of the script is very insecurely based. Only in the most general sense can it be said that the square Aramaic script began to come into use at approximately the time of Ezra, but alongside it the old Hebrew script continued in widespread use, even if in somewhat limited circles, down to the Christian era. We have seen that the evidence of Samaritan orthography and of its textual tradition also point to the Hasmonaean era as marking the decisive development, though in each case the evidence is somewhat ambiguous.

No useful purpose would be served here by examining those cases where dispute has arisen as to the priority of the Samaritan Pentateuch over against the Massoretic Text in those instances where the differences is more than a matter of orthography. The most famous such case is the reading 'Gerizim' for 'Ebal' at Deuteronomy 27:4, and a number of scholars have taken this to be the better reading here;[78] but in most other cases the Massoretic Text is usually favoured. In no instance, however, does it seem likely that agreement on a solution of this kind of difficulty would help to throw light on the problem of dating. The differences usually appear to reflect polemic on one side or the other, and this could have taken place at any point during a very long period.

Finally, we have noticed that Samaritan practice in the matter of the canon of scripture should not be regarded, as it so often has been, as something quite alien from the rest of Judaism. In fact, a wide range of attitudes could be found, and it appears that the Samaritans were similar to the Sadducees and to the Jews of the diaspora at Alexandria in the way in which they accorded fully canonical status to the Torah alone, with a more limited place being found for certain other works.

[78] See Eissfeldt, *The Old Testament: an Introduction*, pp. 216, 695. NEB has 'Ebal' in the text and 'Gerizim' as a footnote.

## The Samaritans and Other Groups within Judaism

We have just observed that Samaritan practice with regard to the canon of scripture places them within the broad spectrum of Judaism in this respect. A comparable state of affairs has been noted in various aspects of religious belief and practice. It therefore remains to consider just what can be known of the relation, both of similarity and dissimilarity, between the Samaritans and other Jewish groups. It has long been recognized that the description by Josephus of Judaism as being comprised of 'three schools of thought . . . which held different opinions concerning human affairs' *(Ant.* XIII, 171), the Pharisees, the Sadducees and the Essenes, is a serious over-simplification—for whatever purpose. He himself later introduces a fourth group, the Zealots, and it has come to be recognized in recent years that the complexities and ramifications of Judaism at this period were much greater than had previously been thought.

This recognition has, of course, largely been due to the discovery of the Qumran scrolls, and an interesting side-light is thrown upon it by the variety of identifications which has been proposed for the Qumran covenanters. One work, for example, has devoted a whole section to considering suggested identifications that have been made between the covenanters and Essenes, Sadducees, Samaritans and Christians.[79] In every case there are points of similarity sufficient to have persuaded competent scholars to suggest an identification, though only the Essene link has been at all widely accepted. The point is that we should be reminded by these uncertainties that there is an overlapping and a complexity about the different groups that made up the Judaistic world that should warn against any facile identifications. With these provisos in mind, it will be useful to observe some of the similarities between the Samaritans and certain other groups, not in order to suggest an identification, but in order to illustrate once again how the Samaritans fit within a Judaistic context. In particular, similarities with the Sadducees and with the Qumran covenanters will claim our attention.

[79] M. Burrows, *More Light on the Dead Sea Scrolls* (London, 1958), Part V, pp. 253ff.

Links between the Samaritans and the Sadducees were noted already by Montgomery, who, thinking as he did in terms of a much earlier schism, explained 'this close relationship in theology and practice... by the supposition of the maintenance of intercourse between the priests of Jerusalem and of Shechem'.[80] If, however, it is no longer axiomatic to think in terms of an earlier schism, a simpler explanation may be sought in the fact that, within the broad spectrum of Judaism, the Sadducees and the Samaritans each represented similar interests, conservative in nature and priestly dominated, but differing as to the true locus of the priestly cultus. This provides a satisfactory explanation of those links between the two groups which have already been observed—denial of resurrection of the dead, strictness as to Sabbath-observance, and the limitation of the Canon of Scripture to the Pentateuch, all of which can be regarded as characteristically conservative emphases, distrustful of anything which might be regarded as an innovation. Other similarities noted by Montgomery (concerning levirate marriage, and concerning the disposal of an animal that had died a natural death) may again have their roots in a similarly conservative tradition of Pentateuchal interpretation.[81] Striking also is the way in which Samaritans and Sadducees could be joined together in condemnation in the Mishnah. Thus, in the matter of the ritual cleanliness of women, the Tractate Niddah, already quoted concerning Samaritan women,[82] immediately continues: 'The daughters of the Sadducees, if they follow after the ways of their fathers, are deemed like to the women of the Samaritans; but if they have separated themselves and follow after the ways of the Israelites, they are deemed like to the women of the Israelites.'[83] Comparisons of this nature clearly do not imply any detailed likenesses, but they do suggest that both groups could be considered to be in an analogous relationship to what came to be orthodox Judaism. It is not necessarily a case of direct influence or borrowing, but both groups display similar tendencies within the total picture of Judaism. In this connection it is relevant to notice the way in which Samaritans and Sadducees are associated in a number of early Christian references. Thus they are linked in

---

[80] Montgomery, op. cit., p. 72.
[81] Montgomery, op. cit., p. 187.          [82] Above, p. 139.
[83] Niddah, 4.2 (Danby's edition, p. 748).

Ps-Tertullian, *Adversus omnes Haereses*, while in the *Clementine Recognitions* (1, 54), Dositheus is made a Sadducee. To some extent these connections may be due to a tendency to lump all heresies together, yet the particular association is striking.[84]

The other obvious area for consideration concerning links between the Samaritans and the Sadducees is the priesthood, which we have already seen as playing an important part in Judaeo-Samaritan divisions. If it was indeed the case that the division between the communities was particularly associated with differing priestly claims, then the links between Samaritans and Sadducees would be the more readily understood. The precise origin of the term 'Sadducee', and the date at which the group emerged, are matters of continuing dispute, but it is incontestable that they were the priestly aristocracy in Jerusalem at the beginning of the Christian era. It is at least possible that it was in the claims that they made for Jerusalem as against the Samaritans' claims for Shechem that the only sharp distinction between the two groups lay, and that for the Samaritans the position of Jerusalem was weakened by its lack of antiquity compared with their own holy place. The description of the establishment of Jerusalem in Chronicle II certainly gives such an impression.

Precision in matters of this kind cannot be reached, and we must simply note the very extensive area of similarity between the two groups. When we come to make comparisons between the Samaritans and the Qumran covenanters, the points of contact are, as might be expected, rather different. Here again, though, it will be parallels rather than direct influence which will concern us—a point stressed by Bowman in his study of this inter-relationship.[85] As with the Sadducees, some parallels may be noted in regard to the priesthood, though in a somewhat different way. Both the Samaritans and the Qumran community laid stress upon the importance of a properly constituted priesthood, and both claimed that they possessed the true priesthood, disparaging thereby the

---

[84] These and other similar passages are discussed by Caldwell, art. cit. See also J. Danielou, *The Theology of Jewish Christianity* (London, 1964), pp. 69–72.

[85] Bowman, 'Die Samaritaner und die Sekte von Qumran', in *Samaritanische Probleme*. See also his article, 'Contact between Samaritan Sects and Qumran?', *VT*, 7, 1957, pp. 184–9.

claims of the contemporary Jerusalem hierarchy. As has been seen already, however, a certain amount of difficulty arises at this point.[86] While the importance at Qumran of a Zadokite priesthood is well-established, the evidence that a similar requirement was characteristic of the Samaritans is less clear; and though Bowman has argued forcefully for such a link, those who have reviewed his works on the subject have noted that the association is often referred to but never properly clarified.[87] The link between the Qumran sect and the Samaritans at this point, therefore, is probably better seen in negative terms—a common rejection of the claims of the Jerusalem hierarchy—than in positive ones—common stress on the Zadokite line.

Something similar can be said with regard to the more general attitude to Jerusalem. Some attention has already been given to the relevant Qumran material,[88] and of course for the Samaritans the Jerusalem Temple was the direct result of the schism instigated by Eli. An important part of the Samaritan Chronicle II, which replaces 2 Samuel 7, is that which describes the letter of the Samaritan High-Priest Jair to David, warning him against his design of building a Temple at Jerusalem and explaining that the temple and the divine presence could not be in any place but in the chosen place Mount Gerizim Bethel (Sam. Chr. II, 2 Sam. B, I*), whereupon David abandoned the project. As elsewhere in Samaritan writings, there is some approval of David but none for Jerusalem. Yet this again is a negative form of agreement, for while they had it in common that Jerusalem was not the chosen place, the Qumran sect and the Samaritans clearly differed as to what should replace it.

Another link, perhaps also to be associated with this common concern for a true priesthood, is the way in which both groups make much use of the idea of the great divide between the children of light and the children of darkness, each regarding themselves as alone the children of light, the favoured ones, while all else had come under the influence and teaching of Belial. In both cases the natural consequence of this was an elaborate concern for

[86] Cf. above, pp. 143f.
[87] See the review of *Samaritanische Probleme* by Sir Godfrey Driver in *JTS*, NS, XX, 1969, p. 269.
[88] Above, p. 141.

maintaining purity, with very precise purification rituals. Each also looked forward to the coming of a Moses-like messianic figure, based on their exegesis of Deut. 18:18. Then would be revealed those who were truly the sons of light and God's favoured ones.

Bowman has also argued for a number of other links, the genuineness of which will not be beyond dispute. This is certainly the case with his suggestion that each community had its own interpretation of the figure of the *nāsi'*, prince, found in the later chapters of Ezekiel, and of the restored Temple of Ezekiel 40–48. As we have seen more than once already, both the origin and the later interpretation of this Ezekiel material is too much disputed for confident interpretation to be possible. When it comes to more detailed parallels such as the priestly regulations for working out of the calendar, and possible Samaritan parallels with the Qumran Manual of Discipline, we are on firmer ground; even if there is no direct association, we are clearly in the same area of thought.[89]

If more were known of the early history of the Samaritan sects, it might well be that parallels between these groups and the Qumran covenanters would prove even more instructive. Dositheus has been described by a number of authors as introducing a kind of 'Samaritan Essenism',[90] and long before the Qumran discoveries, Montgomery noted features of Dosithean practice which appeared to link them with Essenism—frequent baptisms, scrupulousness with regard to bodily display, fear of contact with others—and pointed out that already in the fourth century A.D. Epiphanius had linked the Essenes with Samaritanism.[91] These points must not be pressed, for they are of far too general a nature for detailed conclusions to be built upon them; they nevertheless help to build up our general picture of the milieu in which Samaritanism had its roots.

In view of parallels of this kind, Bowman's conclusion in his later study, that the Samaritans were by origin 'more a national than a religious group' is surprising.[92] The whole tenor of his argument

---

[89] Bowman, *Samaritanische Probleme*, esp. p. 94.
[90] Danielou, op. cit., p. 72; cf. Caldwell, art. cit., p. 116.
[91] Montgomery, op. cit., p. 263.
[92] *Samaritanische Probleme*, p. 86. His earlier article, 'Contact between the Samaritan Sects and Qumran?,' had expressed the matter more satisfactorily.

seems rather to point to Samaritanism as emerging from the religious background of the last pre-Christian centuries, and even if they did maintain and embody some distinctively northern traditions, this should certainly not be taken to imply distinct ethnic origins. Indeed, the references to the Samaritans from within rabbinic Judaism convey a similar impression. Just as Josephus had noted that the Samaritans sometimes claimed affinity with the Jews and sometimes repudiated them, so a similar attitude can be detected on the part of the Jews towards the Samaritans. In the Mishnah, as we have seen, they are linked with the Sadducees as a group which should have known better but had nevertheless fallen away; and it was to their return, rather than to any vengeance against them, that Judaism in the early Christian centuries looked forward. Later, of course, attitudes hardened much more, but it is clear that final links were not broken until well into the Christian era.

# 6

# Summary and Conclusions

This survey began by noting the fact that until the early years of
the present century it was assumed that Samaritan origins could be
traced back to the eighth century B.C., and that the later Samaritans
were the descendants of the aliens settled in Israel by the Assyrian
conquerors. More recently a different 'accepted historical framework' has emerged. The phrase is that of N. H. Snaith, who regards
the 'schism' as having taken place between the time of Ezra and that
of Alexander the Great.[1] We have already noted that this fourth-
century period was indeed an important one in the history of the
community centred on Mount Gerizim, but that is not to say
that some specific event which can be labelled a 'schism' took
place at that time. Another part of this 'accepted historical
framework' which needs to be questioned is that which identifies
the Samaritans with those Palestinians who had never been
driven out of the country into exile, for here again we have seen
that this assumption is gratuitous—there is nothing in the references to those who remained in the land which would connect
them with the Samaritans by way of religious practice or even
geography.

It would seem, then, that this historical framework should not
be accepted, any more than the older view of an eighth-century
breach. Both the Samaritan dating of their dispute with the Jews
in the time of Eli, and the Jewish version placing the separation in
the eighth century, are to be regarded as examples of a later polemic
of the kind which takes the view that 'the devil sinneth from the

[1] In H. M. Orlinsky and N. H. Snaith, 'Studies in the Second Part
of the Book of Isaiah', *VTS*, 14, p. 221.

beginning'; neither presentation is historically acceptable. Again, the attempts made by some modern scholars to pinpoint a schism at various dates within the Old Testament period have not carried conviction. The only significant historical event which we are able to trace is the building of the Temple on Mount Gerizim, and—while this will hardly have smoothed relationships among the different groups within Judaism—it need not of itself have precipitated any decisive breach.

The picture which emerges is not of some sudden and dramatic event which divided Jews and Samaritans irrevocably. Rather, Samaritanism is part of that larger complex which constitutes the Judaism of the last pre-Christian centuries. With all this in mind, the appropriateness of the word 'schism' to describe the deterioration in relations between the communities is doubtful. It may indeed be the case that the regular use of this word in describing Samaritan origins is itself an example of the remarkable success of anti-Samaritan polemic and the way in which it has affected the interpretation of the Old Testament material. For the whole idea of a schism, as Ackroyd has pointed out, requires an orthodox norm, and such a norm was not established in Judaism until the Christian era. In these circumstances, no one group within the rich complex of Judaism should be regarded as schismatic.[2] The word and ideas associated with it retain a pejorative force in English, and once we begin to think in terms of a schism, we begin also to think in terms of abuses that might have caused it, and thereby the allegation of foreign and pagan origins, or of syncretistic practices, are given credence, and a kind of dossier against the Samaritans is built up. The simple truth is, as it is hoped that the first main part of this study has shown, that there is no reference to the Samaritans in the Hebrew Old Testament. Some of the allusions in the work of the Chronicler may point to a situation which would later develop into Judaeo-Samaritan hostility, but that is the most that can be said.

If the Old Testament evidence is negative, however, that from a later period has much to tell us. There are frequent allusions to the Samaritans from the book of Ecclesiasticus onward, and recent research into the characteristic features of Samaritanism has made it possible to place the community within the rich variety

[2] Ackroyd, *Israel under Babylon and Persia*, p. 185.

of the Judaism of this period. Here again, there is a danger that standards imported from the study of the history of the Christian church might be misleadingly applied to Judaism. Just as 'schism' has pejorative overtones, so in Christianity—at least since about the third century A.D.—a 'catholic' or 'orthodox' norm has usually been regarded as desirable, and deviations from such a norm have been regarded as regrettable, even if at times they were understandable. It is not easy to make the transference from this position to one in which a wide variety of belief and practice within certain rather loosely defined norms was entirely acceptable. (The old adage about Judaism requiring orthopraxy rather than orthodoxy is relevant here, provided only that due allowance is made for the great variety of 'praxis' that might still continue.) This variety is clear from the Old Testament itself, and might be illustrated by the very varied attitudes shown to those outside the covenant-community—varied attitudes sometimes found within one book, and certainly in the contrasts between, say, Esther on the one hand and Ruth and Jonah on the other. At a later date the variety of eschatological beliefs as between Pharisees and Sadducees affords another illustration. Within these and other variations, Samaritan beliefs and practice can be seen as one expression, rather than as something altogether alien.

We conclude, therefore, that all the evidence suggests that the decisive formative period for Samaritanism was the epoch from the third century B.C. to the beginning of the Christian era; and that it emerged from the matrix of Judaism during this time, with some measure of communication continuing well into the Christian era between Samaritans and various Jewish groups. The characteristic Samaritan emphases were conservative—an anxiety to retain the old faith rather than to launch out into new and uncharted areas, and in one sense this has been the strength and the weakness of Samaritanism ever since. There is no evidence that any one decisive event played a special part in widening the breach between Jews and Samaritans. What is clear is that differences concerning the priesthood and the true sanctuary were among those that did most to ensure that reconciliation was unlikely.

In recent years, some measure of reconciliation has been achieved, not least because of the sympathetic interest shown in Samaritanism by Israeli scholars. This has been part of a general renewal of interest, and a few of the conclusions of some modern scholars have been examined here. (Much of this revival of interest has centred on later Samaritanism, which has not been our concern in this study.) Even where agreement with some of these views has not been possible, the breadth of this interest is still greatly to be welcomed, since only through such a revival of interest—coinciding to some extent as it has with a revival in the fortunes of the present-day survivors of the community—can justice be done to a group who have so often been unjustly maligned.

# Index of Biblical References

## Old Testament

# Index of Authors